ONE

SKEWERED, ROLLED, TIED & STUFFED

When you yearn for greater than only a undeniable roast or chop

, choose up your knife, seize your ball of butcher's twine, and discover ways to maneuver past the fundamentals of butchery. At the Fatted Calf, we pleasure ourselves on making succulent skewers, filled birds and beasts, and pro roasts that variety from the traditional to the unusual. These specialties are as stunning to behold as they may be to take pleasure in on the table. Mastering a handful of nifty talents will let you butcher, season, cook, and carve with flourish. Those techniques, blended with marinades and seasonal stuffings, will assist you to raise easy hunks of meat to mind-blowing centerpieces for all occasions.

Skewered

Cooking meat on skewers is sort of as vintage as lights a fire. It is difficult to face up to the historical appeal of meat on a stick. Quick and versatile, it's far best for feeding as few as or as many as twenty.

Most cuts of meat, from duck breast to goat legs, may be skewered. Although lean and smooth cuts are frequently favored, even the ones cuts now no longer historically related to high-warmth grilling, including shoulder cuts of red meat, pork, goat, or lamb, can paintings similarly well. They are flavorful, particularly while marinated in advance of time, and when you have now no longer misplaced the

capacity to chunk your food, they may be a terrific preference for skewering. Avoid the use of overly difficult cuts with an abundance of connective tissue, including shank and neck cuts. Cut or dice the beef into similar-length portions, typically 1 to 1½ inches (2.five to four cm), to make sure uniform cooking. You need lots of floor place for browning (which improves flavor), however the portions need to now no longer be so small which you lose the juicy, succulent center. Season the beef earlier than skewering to permit the flavors to develop. For leaner meats, some hours will suffice. For greater sturdy cuts (including lamb or red meat shoulder), an afternoon or is best.

A style of alternatives exist for spearing any meat, from bamboo sticks to lengths of sugarcane. Although maximum are simply a car for the beef, some, inclusive of lemongrass or robust herb stems, are intended to impart flavor. Reusable chrome steel skewers are favored for maximum jobs. Because they're right warmness conductors, they velocity the cooking, and in contrast to timber skewers, they by no means splinter or burn. That said, bamboo skewers truely have their vicinity, specifically at events or across the campfire. To save you the uncovered timber on bamboo or different timber skewers from burning, soak them in bloodless water to cowl for at the least a 1/2 of hour earlier than threading meat onto them, and make sure to put a chunk of meat over the top of every skewer.

When you're almost prepared to skewer, get rid of the pro meat from the fridge to mood for approximately a 1/2 of hour. Just as with steaks or roasts, tempering the beef (that is, bringing it to room temperature) allows it to prepare dinner dinner greater flippantly. If you're the usage of timber skewers, make sure they had been soaked in water earlier than skewering. Thread the portions of meat via their middle or thickest component onto the skewer, spacing them at the least 1 inch (2.five cm) apart. Although it could appearance greater attractive to have the beef portions tightly packed at the skewer, spacing them generously allows the beef to brown greater very well and prepare dinner dinner greater flippantly. Likewise, readorning your meaty skewers with a cornucopia of seasonal veggies makes them quite and colorful, however meats and veggies seldom prepare dinner dinner on the identical charge and need to be skewered separately. If you're cooking special cuts at the identical skewer, make sure to select cuts with the intention to prepare dinner dinner at greater or much less the identical charge. More sensitive cuts, inclusive of lean poultry, rabbit, or organ meats, advantage

from a shielding layer of fats wrapped round
every piece. Caul fats or thinly sliced bacon or pancetta works properly. Thread oddly fashioned or unwieldy portions of meat onto parallel skewers to save you the beef from flopping round throughout cooking.

Although you may prepare dinner dinner skewers beneathneath a broiler or in a grill pan, there's no actual alternative for grilling over a hearthplace outdoors. Cook skewered meats over exceptionally excessive warmness, round 550°F (290°C), or kind of the identical temperature you will use for a steak or chop. If you're grilling over charcoal, vicinity your skewers at the grill the instant the flames die down, leaving energetic coals that radiate a massive quantity of warmness. Turn your skewers each minute or with the intention to brown on all sides. Skewers prepare dinner dinner quickly, maximum of them taking no greater than eight to ten minutes.

PORK BROCHETTES WITH HERBES DE PROVENCE

The captivating heady fragrance of those red meat morsels, crusted in black pepper, white pepper, and herbes de Provence, is tough to withstand because it wafts off the grill. These brochettes, a summertime favored on the Fatted Calf, are an incredible preference for a massive gathering. The recipe can without problems be doubled or tripled, and the beef may be pro properly in advance.

SERVES 6
2½ pounds (1.2 kg) boneless red meat picnic, reduce into 1½-inch (four cm) cubes
2½ teaspoons first-rate sea salt
four cloves garlic, gently crushed
yellow onion, sliced ½ inch (12 mm) thick
tablespoons olive oil
½ teaspoon black peppercorns
¼ teaspoon white peppercorns
2 tablespoons Herbes de Provence

Season the red meat with the salt. In a massive bowl, integrate the garlic, onion, and olive oil. Add the pro red meat and flip to coat flippantly.

In a spice grinder, integrate the peppercorns and herbs and grind finely. Dust the aggregate over the red meat, then blend to coat flippantly. Cover and refrigerate for at the least 1 day and ideally for two to three days. If you're marinating for longer than 1 day, make sure to combine the red meat as soon as an afternoon to redistribute the seasonings.

Prepare a medium-warm hearthplace in a charcoal grill. Thread the red meat cubes onto skewers, spacing them approximately 1 inch (2.five cm) apart. Discard the onions, garlic, and different remnants of the marinade. Grill the skewers, turning frequently, for eight to ten minutes, till flippantly browned on all sides.

Alternatively, prepare dinner dinner the skewers beneathneath a preheated broiler, turning them frequently, the usage of the identical timing.

Harissa-Marinated Lamb Kebabs

HARISSA-MARINATED LAMB KEBABS

Harissa is a North African warm sauce used to boost quite a few dishes, meaty and otherwise. Although it also includes served as a condiment along food, it additionally makes a splendidly highly spiced marinade for fuller-flavored meats which include goat, beef, or lamb. If you're a spice fiend, blend up a touch more harissa to drizzle over your skewers on the table. Serve the kebabs over couscous

or wrapped in flatbread, observed with grilled veggies and

lemon-scented yogurt sauce.

SERVES 6
2½ pounds (1.2 kg) boneless lamb leg, reduce into 1½-inch (four cm) cubes
2½ teaspoons first-class sea salt
HARISSA
1 teaspoon cumin seeds, toasted and floor 1 teaspoon freshly floor black pepper
1½ teaspoons overwhelmed dried Aleppo pepper 1½ teaspoons unsmoked Spanish paprika
½ teaspoon floor cayenne
½ yellow onion, sliced ¼ inch (6 mm) thick
three cloves garlic, overwhelmed 1 tablespoon olive oil

In a huge bowl, season the lamb with the salt and blend well.

To make the harissa, in a small bowl, integrate the cumin, black pepper, Aleppo pepper, paprika, cayenne, onion, garlic, and olive oil and stir to incorporate. Pour the harissa over the pro lamb and blend well. Cover tightly and refrigerate for at the least 1 day and ideally for two to a few days. If you're marinating for longer than 1 day, make sure to combine the lamb as soon as an afternoon to redistribute the seasonings.

Prepare a medium-warm hearthplace in a charcoal grill. Thread the lamb cubes onto skewers, spacing them approximately 1 inch (2.five cm) apart. Discard the onion, garlic, and different remnants of the marinade. Grill the skewers, turning frequently, for six to eight minutes, till lightly browned on all sides.

Alternatively, prepare dinner dinner the skewers beneathneath a preheated broiler, turning them frequently, the usage of the equal timing.

MARSHA'S GRILLED RABBIT SPIEDINI WITH CHICORIES, OLIVES, AND ALMONDS

This recipe turned into exceeded right all the way down to us from Marsha McBride, chef and proprietress of Berkeley's Café Rouge. Before "sustainability" have become a family phrase and nose-to-tail ingesting have become fashionable, Marsha turned into sourcing first-class meats

from neighborhood farms for her save and the usage of old-global strategies to provide a extensive variety of charcuterie for her restaurant. Many Bay Area butchers and charcutiers labored a spell at Café Rouge, in which certainly considered one among our favourite menu services is that this savory grilled rabbit spiedini (Italian for "skewers") that requires each the beef and the organs of the rabbit, served over a salad of chicories, olives, and almonds.

SERVES FOUR
SPIEDINI
I rabbit, 2 to a few pounds (900 g to I.four kg),boned 2 rabbit kidneys, every halved
I rabbit liver, quartered
Fine sea salt
I teaspoon coriander seeds, toasted and floor
Grated zest of ½ orange
2 tablespoons chopped sparkling flat-leaf parsley 2 tablespoons chopped sparkling thyme
I tablespoon chopped garlic
½ cup (a hundred and twenty ml) more-virgin olive oil
½ cup (a hundred and twenty ml) rosé wine
four skinny slices pancetta, selfmade or storebought
SALAD

¼ cup (60 ml) purple wine
vinegar I shallot, finely minced
Fine sea salt
I tablespoon Dijon mustard
¾ cup (a hundred and eighty ml)
more-virgin olive oil four cups
(eighty g) stemmed arugula
four cups (eighty g) trimmed escarole
hearts four cups (eighty g) trimmed
frisée leaves
¼ cup (forty g) chopped picholine olives
½ cup (fifty five g) chopped toasted
almonds Freshly floor pepper

Cut the rabbit meat into 1-inch (2.five-cm) cubes. Season the beef, kidneys, and liver with salt and the coriander. In a huge bowl, integrate the orange zest, parsley, thyme, garlic, olive oil, and wine and blend well. Add the pro rabbit and blend to coat lightly. Cover and refrigerate overnight.

To make the French dressing for the salad, in a bowl, macerate the shallot withinside the vinegar for some minutes. Add a pinch of salt and the Dijon mustard, then slowly whisk withinside the olive oil to emulsify. Set aside.

Prepare a medium-warm hearthplace in a charcoal grill. Remove the rabbit from the marinade. Have prepared four skewers. Wrap the liver portions with the pancetta. Thread 1 piece of liver and 1 kidney onto every skewer together with one-fourth of the beef, spacing the portions ½ inch (12 mm) apart. Grill the skewers, turning frequently, for eight to ten minutes, till lightly browned on all sides.

To make the salad, in a huge bowl, integrate the arugula, escarole, and frisée, drizzle with the French dressing, and toss to coat the vegetables lightly. Add the olives, almonds, and some grinds of pepper and toss again.

Divide the salad amongst four plates. Place an entire skewer, nonetheless warm, over every salad and serve.

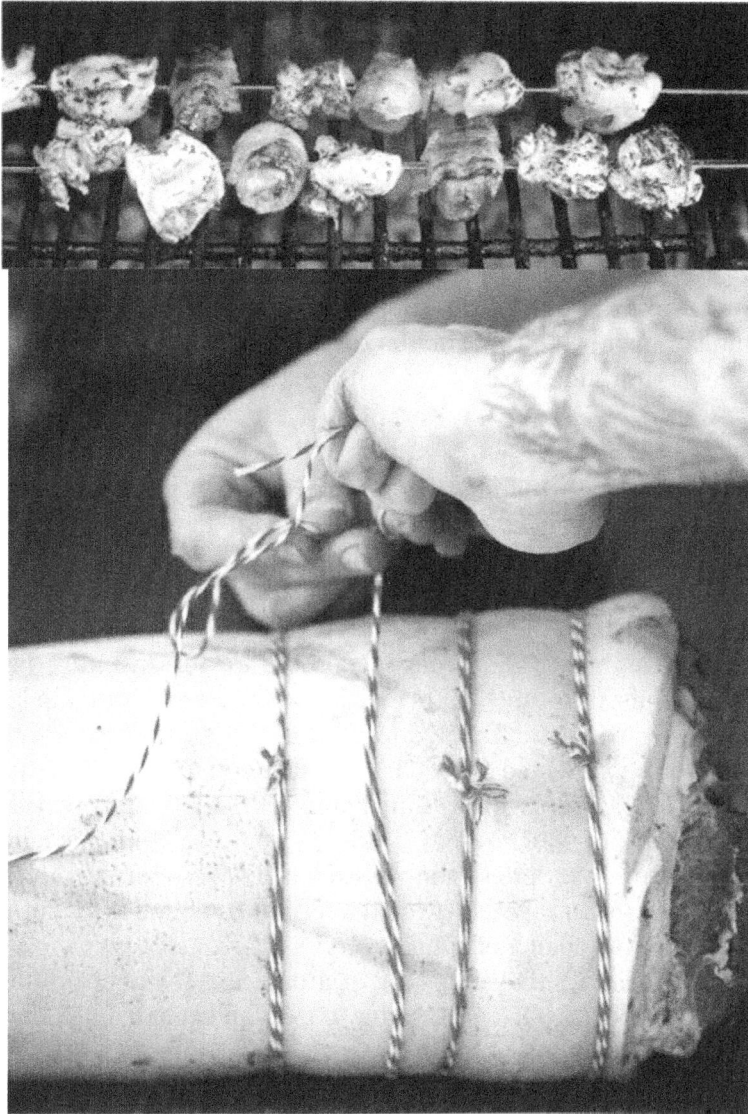

Rolled and Tied

Most huge cuts of meat on the way to be roasted or grilled advantage from being rolled and tied. This creates a uniformly fashioned roast this is simpler to prepare dinner dinner to perfection, carve, and serve. Left au naturel, erratically fashioned cuts or cuts made of numerous smaller muscles, together with red meat shoulder or lamb leg, will prepare dinner dinner erratically and their extremities will generally tend to dry out. On a greater realistic level, tying maintains your seasonings secured while the beef is cooking. And from a cultured factor of view, a rolled and tied roast has a chunk greater expert panache. Attention

to the information of cutting, seasoning, tying, and cooking your hunk of meat will bring about a roast this is as lovely to behold as it's miles scrumptious to eat.

Roasting, Slow Roasting, and Pot Roasting

Roasting, truely defined, approach cooking meat in warm, dry oblique heat, usually in an oven, to provide flavorful caramelization on its floor. You can roast maximum meats, from a fowl to a red meat tenderloin to an entire status pork rib, and what you pick out to roast will dictate the way you roast it.

In general, the usual roasting procedure for an entire hen or a huge reduce of meat (together with a red meat rack or lamb leg) is to get it brown, then flip it down. Sear the roast in a warm oven, commonly preheated to 375°F to 425°F (190°C to 220°C), to brown the outside, then prepare dinner dinner it at a gentler temperature, from 300°F to 350°F (150°F to 180°F), to finish. A stint at a decrease temperature guarantees the roast chefs evenly. For smaller, leaner, or thinner cuts, together with tenderloin, this 2nd segment of low-temperature cooking is unnecessary.

Slow roasting, that's cooking at a decrease temperature, together with 275°F to 325°F (135°C to 165°C), for an extended length of time, without or with an preliminary warm sear, achieves a extraordinary effect. A reduce with a few fats and connective tissue, together with a lamb shoulder or red meat Boston butt, may be sluggish roasted for numerous hours till it's miles very well cooked however nonetheless juicy, extraordinarily soft, and almost falling off the bone.

Pot roasting makes use of a deeper vessel to keep moisture, which makes it just like braising, aleven though with a single, huge reduce of meat. You can both simmer the beef in its very own juices or upload liquid to the pot to facilitate the cooking. Tougher, greater sinewy cuts, together with shank and shoulder, grow to be meltingly soft while pot roasted.

Readying Your Roast

Season nicely and season early! Some humans worry that salt, even a restricted amount, will dry out a roast. True, salt does draw moisture from meat, however after a length of time, way to opposite osmosis, the cells reabsorb a whole lot of that moisture together with the salt and anything different aromatics had been used to season, ensuing in greater flavorful

meat. Salt additionally allows to melt the proteins in meat, making the beef greater soft. Large cuts, cuts with a terrific little bit of fats, meat at the bone, and dense or sinewy cuts significantly advantage from seasoning an afternoon or beforehand. More soft cuts, boneless cuts, smaller or thinner cuts, or cuts with little or no fats can nonetheless be pro beforehand however want to take a seat down for only some hours. The salt in a marinade or dry rub allows the switch of the flavors to the indoors of the beef. A smear of rendered fats or olive oil will assist seasoning adhere and offer a bit shielding coating and browning ammunition for leaner cuts.

All Tied Up

Not each roast desires tying. Many are evidently ideal to seasoning and popping in an oven, together with red meat loin and different bone-in cuts which have their very own integrated structural supports. But roasts which have been butterflied and pro, are stuffed, or have an abnormal form require a chunk of reassembly and securing with butcher's wire. This guarantees that your stuffing doesn't tumble out at some stage in cooking and offers the roast a greater symmetrical form so it chefs greater evenly.

How to Tie a Roast

Start with a terrific spool of one hundred percentage cotton butcher's wire with a minimal twelve-ply thickness (even though 16 ply is higher if you could discover it). Thicker wire is much less probable to snap while you pull it taut. When you're running with wire, you'll need to steady it on your paintings floor to keep away from having it roll over, off, and onto the ground at the same time as you're withinside the center of your coup de grace butcher's knot. Place the ball or cone of wire both on a heavy-bottomed base prepared with a dowel or inner of a small, heavy saucepan.

Lay your pro or crammed roast at the paintings surface. If you're tying a roast with an abnormal shape, tuck in any sticking out bits and pat right into a extra even shape. Have your wire close to at hand.

Leaving one stop connected to the spool, slide the wire under the roast. For a rib roast, plan to knot the wire among the primary and 2nd rib; for a boneless roast, you may make your first knot 2 inches (five cm) or so in from the stop.

To make the primary butcher's knot (additionally referred to as a slip knot), carry the unfastened stop of the wire over pinnacle of the roast. Grab the stop of the wire this is nevertheless connected to the spool with the hoop and pinky arms of your left hand (the string will drape throughout your index and center arms), then drape the unfastened stop of wire over the index and center arms of your left hand (see picturegraph 1 of How to Tie a Roast).

Grab the unfastened stop of wire together along with your proper hand. Then, rotate your left hand in order that your palm is now going through down (see picturegraph 2). Since you're nevertheless conserving the unfastened stop of wire together along with your proper hand, this rotating movement need to shape a loop at the unfastened stop of wire (now no longer the only connected to the spool). Slip the unfastened stop of wire (that's on your proper hand) beneathneath and thru this loop (see picturegraph 3), then flow your left hand out of the manner so that you can tighten the knot (see picturegraph 4). Hold the unfastened piece of wire regular on your proper hand, then tug the stop nevertheless connected to the spool tightly together along with your left hand, till the knot is as tight as possible (see picturegraph five). Make a 2nd, everyday knot on pinnacle of the primary one to make sure that the primary one doesn't loosen (see picturegraph 6), then reduce the wire immediately above the second one knot (see picturegraph 7).

Repeat till the roast is snugly tied. For a rib roast, tie the wire in among every rib. For a boneless roast, repeat the knot at everyday 2inch (five cm) intervals (see picturegraph 8).

HOW TO TIE A ROAST

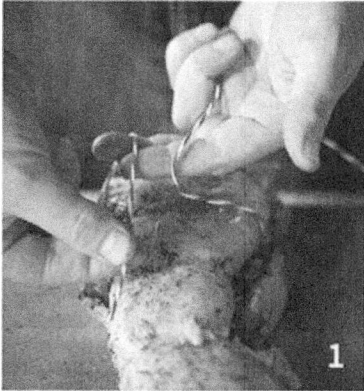

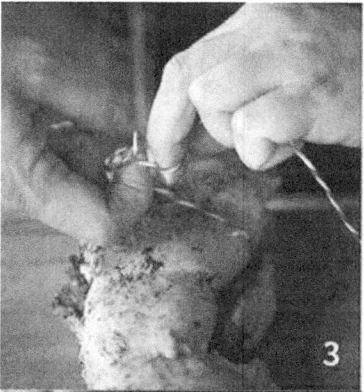

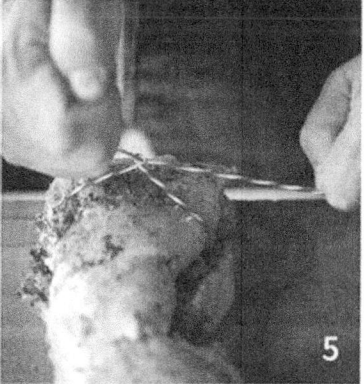

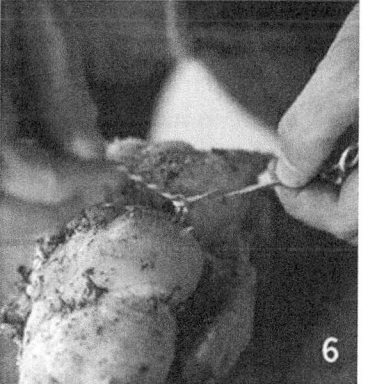

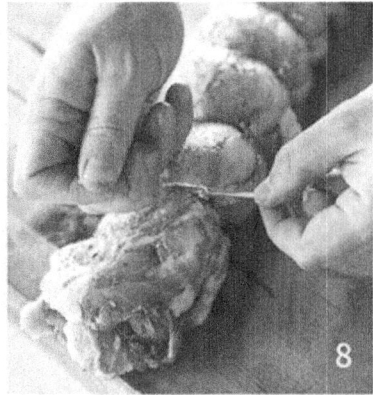

Racks, Pans, and Pots

A stable roasting pan is a superb investment. Heavier pans, ideally crafted from stainless-steel or enameled cast-iron, have a tendency to switch warmness extra efficiently. Choose a pan that may be a bit large than the roast itself. For smaller, leaner roasts, consisting of a beef tenderloin or rack of lamb, the pan does now no longer want to be very deep. For a big or fatty reduce, consisting of a beef center, you may need a deeper pan to gather the drippings.

Almost each roasting recipe you study directs you to outfit the pan with a rack and region the roast at the rack. A rack prevents the roast from sticking to the pan, elevates the roast above the pan drippings, and will increase airflow for extra even roasting. Ideally, the size of the rack nearly suit the ones of the pan, more often than not in your very own safety. If the rack is smaller than the pan, it could slide whilst you take away the pan from the oven, ensuing in hot, sloshing fats which can motive a painful burn. If you do now no longer have a metallic rack, you could style a rack out of vegetables, consisting of leeks or carrots, to assist the roast all through cooking. This vegetable rack may be eaten along the roast or may be milled in conjunction with the drippings for a strong sauce.

Pot roasts want a terrific heavy pan, as well. A deep, enameled castiron braiser or Dutch oven transfers warmness evenly. Choose a pot that may be a bit large than your roast. If the roast is simply too comfortable in its pot, it's going to steam and stew as opposed to gradual roast to a lovely golden brown.

Time and Temperature

All meat, roasts especially, should be allowed to temper, or sit at room temperature, for a spell before cooking. Never transfer a roast directly from the fridge to the oven or you will end up with an overcooked exterior and an undercooked interior. Tempering meat reduces the total cooking time and ensures the meat will cook more evenly. The bigger and denser the roast or cut, the longer you will want to let it temper. A game hen may only need to temper for a half hour, but a bone-in pork shoulder roast should sit for a couple of hours.

CALIBRATE YOUR MEATTHERMO METER

Even the first-class meat thermometers can get dropped, banged approximately in a kitchen drawer, or left to overheat at the range pinnacle. It is constantly a terrific concept to test to ensure that your meat thermometer is nicely calibrated, or studying temperatures accurately. Bring a pot of water to a boil at the range pinnacle. Fill a tumbler with ice cubes and upload bloodless water simply to cowl the cubes. Place the probe stop of the thermometer into the pot of boiling water. It need to study 212°F (100°C). If now no longer, make a minute adjustment with needle-nostril pliers, cautiously turning the nut at the bottom of the thermometer, placed wherein the face meets the probe. Then plunge the probe into the ice water. If it does now no longer check in 32°F (0°C), make some other small adjustment till it reads correctly.

We don't advocate the use of virtual instant-study thermometers. They are hard to calibrate, aleven though a few do have a "reset" button.

We are regularly asked, how lengthy will it take to prepare dinner dinner this roast? The sincere solution is the solution that nobody ever desires to hear: We without a doubt don't know. We can best guess. When did you get rid of the roast from the fridge and what temperature is the beef while you positioned it withinside the oven? Is your oven flawlessly calibrated or does it run warm or cool? Do you have a still oven or a convection oven? Is your oven gas or electric? Will you be opening the oven door every few minutes or are you more of a set-it-and-forget-it kind of cook? Do you like a little pink in your meat or are you a fan of crispy end bits? How you respond to all of these questions affect the equation.

Along with tempering, matters will assist to make certain an ideal piece of cooked meat nearly each time. The first is easy however nonnegotiable. Buy a meat thermometer, discover ways to use it, contend with it, and hold it calibrated and you'll don't have any unsightly surprises— no uncooked chook breasts or depressingly overdone legs of lamb. Meat is costly. Don't depart it to chance. We were cooking meat professionally for almost twenty years, and we nonetheless use a meat thermometer each day. The 2nd manner to enhance your meat cooking abilities is to exercise. Not anybody is born with razor-sharp culinary instincts. The extra you exercise roasting (and the use of your meat thermometer), the extra attuned you'll be to the look, smell, and experience of a superbly cooked roast.

Grilling a Roast

When it's far too warm to show at the oven, while the extraordinary outside beckons, or while there are simply too many chefs withinside the kitchen, take your roast out of doors and prepare dinner dinner it at the grill. A roast cooked at the grill will take a chunk longer, however the publicity to the impossible to resist fragrance of wooden smoke makes the time spent worthwhile.

Use the identical ideas you will use to prepare dinner dinner your roast in a traditional oven. Unlike barbecuing, which requires cooking at a totally low temperature (approximately 180°F/85°C) and with a big quantity of smoke to an inner temperature manner past well-done, a grilled roast ought to be seared over pretty warm coals then completed slowly, with best a small quantity of smoke, till it reaches its goal inner temperature. This effects in a roast with a balanced, meaty taste and best a touch of smoke.

Rake the recent coals right into a pile barely large than the diameter of your roast to create a warm spot for searing. Place your pro and tempered roast at once at the grill grate. Place the roast over the recent spot and brown it, turning it regularly, till it's far frivolously coloured on all facets. Once the beef is frivolously and deeply browned, flow it off of the direct warmth and near the grill lid. If you don't have a lid in your grill, a free foil tent or big bowl positioned over the roast will do. Covering the roast exposes all facets of the roast to the trapped warmth of the coals in order that it chefs slowly and frivolously, simply as it might in an oven. Turn the roast each every so often till it reaches the preferred inner temperature.

Give It a Rest

All roasts, extraordinary and small, advantage from a resting duration after roasting and earlier than carving. The uncommon or less-cooked middle may have some moments to trap up way to the assist of carry-over cooking. The outer layer of meat has the possibility to reabsorb a number of the meaty juices. The cease end result is a roast this is extra frivolously cooked, tender, and juicier.

Pancetta-Wrapped Pork Tenderloin

PANCETTA-WRAPPED PORK TENDERLOIN

Delicate red meat tenderloin is the extra-lean meat adjoining to the loin. This tasty, supple little muscle has an inclination to dry out speedy throughout cooking and might pass from flawlessly crimson to dry and mealy the second one you switch your again at the sauté pan. Our answer is to offer the tenderloin with a defensive layer of much-wanted fats withinside the shape of rich, salty pancetta. As the

tenderloin roasts, the pancetta crisps, basting the tilt muscle with its fats in order that it stays wet and infusing it with its strong taste. The tenderloin is pictured right here with roasted radicchio, an top notch accompaniment.

SERVES 2 OR THREE

1 trimmed red meat tenderloin, approximately 1 pound (450 g) Fine sea salt and freshly floor pepper

¼ cup (fifty five g) Dijon

mustard 2 tablespoons

white wine

three to four tablespoons (approximately 10 g) finelychopped sparkling rosemary About 2 ounces (fifty five g) thinly sliced pancetta, home made or store-bought

Preheat the oven to 425°F (220°C).

Season the tenderloin on all aspects with salt and pepper. In a small bowl, stir collectively the mustard and wine. Using a pastry brush or your hands, cowl the tenderloin liberally with the mix. Sprinkle the rosemary flippantly over the roast.

Lay a 10-inch (25 cm) rectangular sheet of waxed paper or parchment paper on a piece surface. Neatly cowl the paper with the pancetta slices, overlapping them via way of means of approximately ½ inch (12 mm). Lay the tenderloin 1 inch (2.five cm) in from the threshold of the sheet closest to you, putting it parallel to the threshold. Fold the lowest 1 inch (2.five cm) over the tenderloin, after which roll the paper across the tenderloin. The pancetta need to be tightly wrapped across the tenderloin. Remove the paper.

Outfit a baking sheet or a roasting pan with a rack, and vicinity the roast at the rack. Roast for approximately 20 minutes, till the pancetta is golden and crisp and a meat thermometer inserted into the middle of the thickest a part of the roast registers 140°F (60°C).

Remove from the oven and allow relaxation for five to ten minutes. Slice into rounds 1 inch (2.five cm) thick.

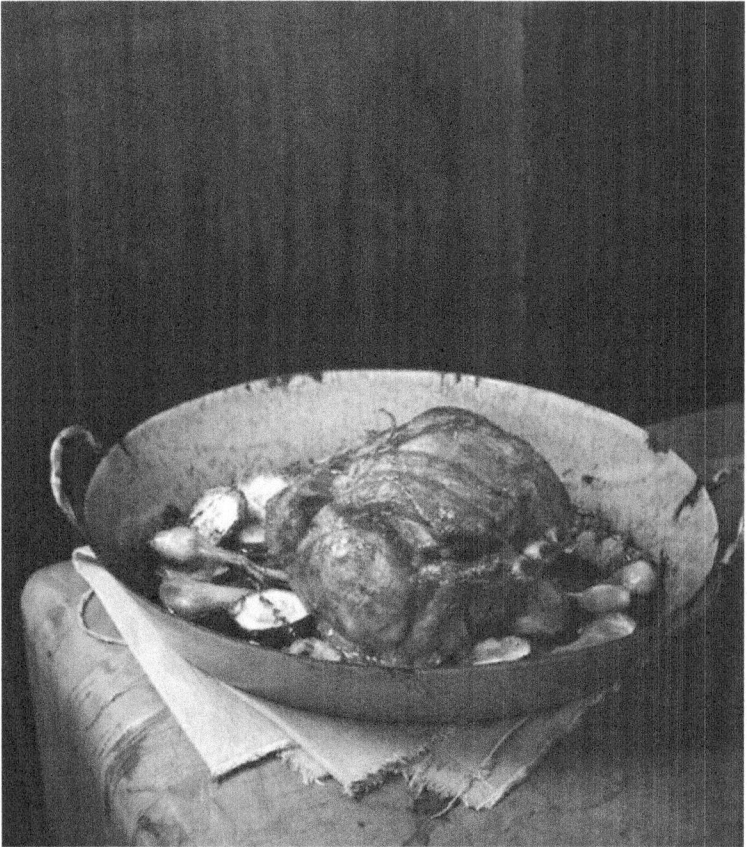

Pork Country Rib with Sherry, Garlic, Thyme, and Pimentón

PORK COUNTRY RIB WITH SHERRY, GARLIC, THYME, AND PIMENTÓN

Pimentón is Spanish for paprika, the intensely purple spice crafted from floor dried peppers. The splendid pimentón de los angeles Vera, from the La Vera valley withinside the Extremadura area of western Spain, is made via way of means of striking the nearby candy and spicy

red peppers from the rafters of large smokehouses, where they gently dry over fires of holm oak. The resulting ground *pimentón* is classified either as *dulce* (sweet), *agridulce* (medium-hot), or *picante* (hot). All three make a perfect seasoning for pork. Use whichever level of heat you find most satisfying. The country rib works particularly well in this preparation because its natural pocket directly behind its ribs allows you to season the meat with the *pimentón* from within.

SERVES FOUR
1 pork country rib roast, about 2½ pounds(1 kg)
2 tablespoons dry sherry
Sea salt
three tablespoons pimentón de los
angeles Vera eight cloves garlic,
sliced paper-thin
2 tablespoons chopped clean thyme

Butterfly the country rib by making a cut directly behind the ribs from the top to the bottom. Using a pastry brush or the tips of your fingers, brush the roast inside and out with the sherry, then sprinkle salt over the entirety of the roast. Lay the roast fat side down on the cutting board and open it like a book. Coat the inside of the roast with the *pimentón*, seasoning from on high so that it disperses more evenly. Next, shingle the garlic slices on the inside of the roast opposite the ribs, followed by a shower of the thyme.

Tie the roast with butcher's cord, making knots in among every rib in addition to one throughout the loin (see How to Tie a Roast). Wrap the roast tightly in plastic wrap and refrigerate overnight.

Remove the roast from the fridge and permit it to mood for approximately 1 hour. Preheat the oven to 375°F (190°C). Outfit a roasting pan with a rack.

Place the roast at the rack, then vicinity withinside the oven for 30 to forty minutes, till well browned. Turn down the warmth to 300°F (150°C) and roast till a thermometer inserted into the thickest a part of the roast farfar from bone registers 140°F (60°C).

Remove from the oven and allow relaxation for 10 to fifteen minutes. Cut away the cord and slice the roast among every rib.

Rabbit Porchetta

RABBIT PORCHETTA

Porchetta is commonly crafted from an entire hog or complete red meat middle, boned, pro generously with garlic, fennel, and herbs, then rolled, tied, and roasted. It is a component of beauty, a amazing large component, pleasant cooked for a large, hungry crowd. This miniature version, made with rabbit, follows the conventional porchetta standards of rolling a roast with spices, garlic, citrus, and herbs. While nonetheless loaded with porchetta flavor, it's miles scaled

for normal eating and may be organized in a fragment of the

time.

SERVES 6

I complete rabbit, four to six pounds (1.eight to 2.7 kg)
2 cloves garlic, pounded to a paste in a mortar
Grated zest of two lemons
Sea salt and freshly floor pepper
three tablespoon fennel pollen
½ cup (30 g) chopped combined clean herbs (together with rosemary, oregano, flat-leaf parsley, and sage)
four tablespoons extra-virgin olive oil

Completely debone the rabbit, following the commands for Whole Boned Rabbit. Lay the boneless rabbit out on a piece floor and rub the interior with the garlic and lemon zest. Season the rabbit outside and inside with salt, pepper, and the fennel pollen, then sprinkle the herbs over the interior. Working lengthwise, roll up the rabbit tightly, then tie with butcher's wire at three-inch (7.five-cm) intervals (see How to Tie a Roast). Wrap the rabbit tightly in plastic wrap and refrigerate for as a minimum 1 day or for up to three days. Remove the roast from the fridge and permit it to mood for 1 hour. Preheat the oven to 425°F (220°C). Outfit a roasting pan with a rack.

Place the rabbit at the rack and rub on all facets with the olive oil. Roast for approximately forty five minutes, till a thermometer inserted into the thickest a part of the rabbit registers 140°F (60°C).

Remove from the oven and allow relaxation for 10 minutes. Slice into rounds
½ inch (12 mm) thick and set up on a platter. Strain the pan juices and spoon over the sliced meat.

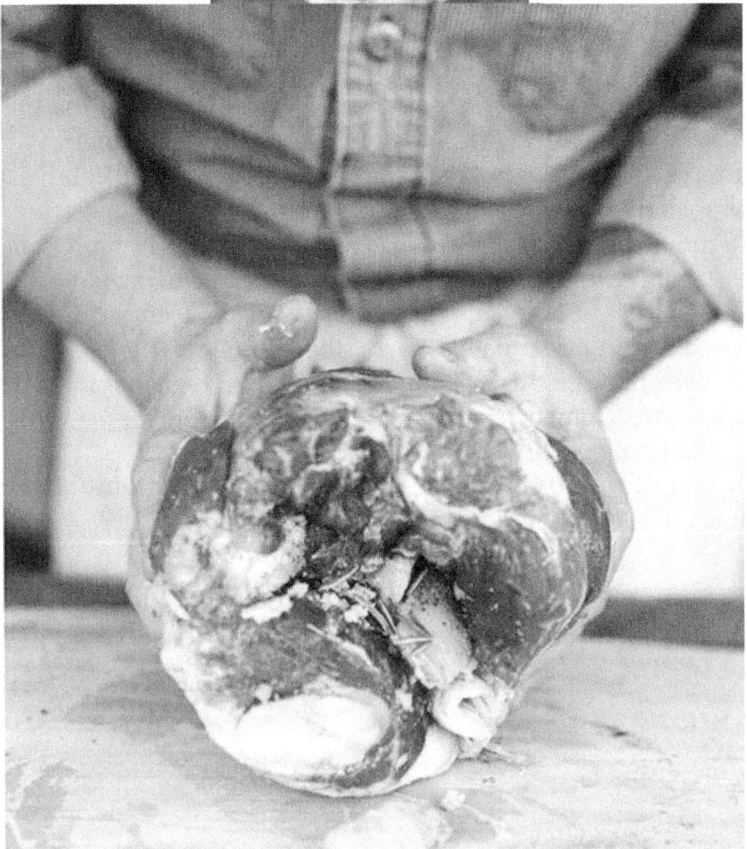

BRASATO AL MIDOLO

In this opulent Tuscan model of pork pot roast, lean, sinewy pork shank is enriched with its very own bone marrow, then simmered in delicately sweet, amber-coloured vin santo. As the roast simmers, the buttery, beefy marrow oozes throughout, flavoring each the beef and the broth encumbered with caramelized shallots—an excellent braise for a cold wintry weather evening! Slice the beef, set up the slices over mashed root veggies or polenta, and pinnacle with the shallots and marrow-enriched sauce.

For ease, ask your butcher to bone the shank and cut up the bone in 1/2 of lengthwise.

SERVES 6

1 complete pork shank, approximately eight pounds (three.6 kg) Fine sea salt and freshly floor pepper

½ cup (15 g) sparkling rosemary needles Sea salt and freshly floor pepper 2 tablespoons extra-virgin olive oil

2 pounds (900 g) shallots or cipollini onions, peeled however left complete

6 cups (1.four L) meat broth, any kind (see Basic Rich Broth) 1 (500-ml) bottle vin santo

Ask your butcher to bone the shank, reducing alongside the herbal seam among the 2 major muscle tissues of the shank to yield a unmarried piece of meat. Then ask that she or he cut up the bone in 1/2 of lengthwise to reveal the marrow.

Season the beef liberally on each facets with salt and pepper. Lay the pork, outside facet down, on a piece floor. Sprinkle the rosemary flippantly over the interior of the shank. Using a butter knife, pry the marrow from the shank bone (keep the bone in your subsequent batch of broth) and set up it lengthwise alongside the middle of the roast. Fold the perimeters of the roast across the marrow to re-create the unique form of the shank and steady with numerous loops of butcher's wire (see How to Tie a Roast). Wrap the roast in plastic wrap and refrigerate in a single day to permit the seasonings to penetrate.

Remove the roast from the fridge and permit it to mood for 1 hour. Preheat the oven to 300°F (150°C).

In a heavy pot or braiser, warmness the olive oil over medium warmness. Add the shank roast and brown properly on all facets. Remove the roast to a platter and set aside. Add the shallots to the pot and sauté for approximately five minutes, till they're golden. Nestle the shank withinside the shallots and upload the broth and wine. The wine and shallots need to attain approximately three-fourths up the manner up the facet of the roast. Bring the liquid to a simmer. Transfer the pot to the oven and prepare dinner dinner the beef slowly,

turning it occasionally, for five to six hours, till it's miles fork-soft and the liquid in all fairness reduced.

You can serve the beef immediately, however like maximum pot roasts, this roast tastes fine if it's miles allowed to relaxation in a single day in its braising liquor. Once the pot has cooled to room temperature, cowl and refrigerate. The following day, switch the bloodless roast to a reducing board. If the fats congealed at the floor of the braising liquid is excessive, take away it. Cut the roast into slices 1¼ inches (three cm) thick and go back the slices to the pot. Heat the pot lightly at the range pinnacle or withinside the oven, then flavor the liquid for seasoning. Serve the recent slices crowned with the marrowrich sauce and shallots.

THE CUBAN

The Cuban

Whole, boneless, pores and skin-on red meat center is a reduce we usually reserve for porchetta, the conventional Italian red meat roast rubbed with garlic, showered with fennel and herbs, then rolled, tied, and roasted till its pores and skin turns mahogany and so crunchy it breaks off into terrifically greasy, impossible-to-face up to shards. The Cuban is a new-global technique to an old-global classic: equal scrumptious red meat center, equal stunning brown and crispy

crackling however pro with a colourful aggregate of cumin, orange, chile, and herbs.

SERVES 10 TO 12
½ pores and skin-on red meat center, 10 to twelve pounds (four.five to five.five kg)
¾ cup (a hundred and seventy g) garlic pounded to a exceptional paste in a mortar Grated zest of one orange
Fine sea salt
2 tablespoons peppercorns, toasted and floor
five allspice berries, toasted and floor
¼ cup (25 g) cumin seeds, toasted and floor
½ cup (55 g) medium-hot (agridulce) pimentón de la Vera
¼ cup (15 g) finely chopped sparkling oregano
¼ cup (15 g) finely chopped sparkling flat-leaf parsley 2 tablespoons extra-virgin olive oil
¼ cup (seventy five g) coarse sea salt

Bone the red meat center following the commands for Whole Boneless Middle. Lay the center on a slicing board and rub the garlic into the meat, ensuring to get into the grooves wherein the ribs had been eliminated and into the pocket wherein the shoulder blade changed into eliminated. Spread the orange zest over the meat, then liberally season with exceptional sea salt observed with the aid of using the pepper, allspice, cumin, *pimentón*, oregano, and parsley.

Although you could tie the roast alone, it's miles simpler to tie it if you could enlist a further set of hands. Roll the loin closer to the lowest of the belly, urgent it tightly as you go. Tie the roast perpendicular to the mild rating marks, the use of double lengths of wire at 2-inch (five cm) intervals (see How to Tie a Roast). Refrigerate the roast exposed or loosely protected with a tea towel for as a minimum 1 day or for up to a few days to permit the flavors of the seasonings to penetrate the meat. Do now no longer wrap in plastic wrap, as moisture trapped among the plastic and the pores and skin can save you the pores and skin from crisping withinside the oven.

Remove the roast from the fridge and permit it to mood for 1 to two hours. Preheat the oven to 375°F (190°C). Outfit a roasting pan with a rack.

Place the roast at the rack. Rub it on all aspects with the olive oil, then sprinkle it calmly with the coarse salt. Transfer to the oven and roast for 30 to forty minutes, till the pores and skin is golden brown and crispy. Turn down the oven temperature to 300°F (150°C) and preserve to prepare dinner dinner till a thermometer inserted into the thickest a part of the loin registers 140°F (60°C). This can take from 2½ to four hours, relying at the thickness of the roast.

Remove from the oven and permit relaxation for as a minimum half-hour earlier than carving. Cut into slices to serve, the use of a serrated knife to reduce via the crunchy outdoors of the pores and skin.

Stuffed

If you need to feature a touch oh là là for your dinner table, keep in mind the opportunity of stuffing your foremost course. Everybody loves to find out the prize inside, specially while that prize is a warm caramelized fig or a fulfilling mouthful of garlicky greens. Stuffings have the introduced advantage of preserving roasts wet, flavorful, and juicy all through cooking.

What to Stuff

The conventional Thanksgiving turkey is the best-recognized

crammed fowl, however severa different birds, from a plump quail to a flavorful guinea hen, are simply ready to be crammed. A entire chicken is preferably constructed for stuffing: the breast chefs a whole lot quicker than the legs, so stuffing the hollow space facilitates to hold the breast wet even as the legs end cooking. Stuffed boneless or in part boneless birds make an fashionable presentation on the table.

Whole beasts along with rabbits, sheep, and hogs also are precise applicants for stuffing. Similar to entire birds, their legs and shoulders prepare dinner dinner at a special price from their middles. Stuffing their belly hollow space facilitates to hold their sensitive loins juicy even as their legs and shoulders end roasting.

In truth, you could stuff nearly any reduce, only for the amusing of it. If it does now no longer have a obviously taking place hollow space to stuff, you could both butterfly it or reduce a small pouch into its center.

Stuffings

Bread stuffings, the type which might be trotted out every vacation season, continually locate themselves on the epicenter of each glad recollections and own circle of relatives feuds. We dare now no longer interfere with tons recommendation or novel concepts. From cornbread to challah, bread stuffings are excellent for maintaining the fowl wet and sopping up the ones scrumptious roasting juices. They may be saved incredibly straightforward, pro with leeks, celery, and herbs, or tarted up with the whole lot from sausage and mushrooms to apples and chestnuts.

Grains, along with rice, *farro*, wheat berries, or couscous, additionally make extremely good stuffings for chicken. They serve tons the equal motive as a bread stuffing, absorbing the extra juice and fats from the fowl because it roasts whilst maintaining the fowl itself wet.

Vegetables, along with cooked greens, leeks, or wild mushrooms, make appealing and flavorful stuffings. In maximum cases, you may need to prepare dinner dinner the veggies completely previous to stuffing, as they'll now no longer prepare dinner dinner sufficiently inner of a roast. Be certain to carve the roast to show a mosaic of stuffing and meat in every slice.

Fruits, chutneys, and mostarde upload taste and texture at the side of moisture to beef roasts. Roasted apples and quince, brandied prunes, chutneys, and mostarde can all be used to stuff a beef loin, us of a rib roast, or shoulder.

Forcemeats and sausage make particularly excellent stuffings for leaner cuts and beasts, along with beef loin, crown roast, rabbit, and smaller chicken. They offer now no longer simply moisture however an amazing little bit of delivered fats. They also can be delivered to bread or grain stuffings. Always make sure to take the inner temperature of a sausage stuffing. It should be cooked to as a minimum 140°F (60°C) to be appropriately eaten, no matter the temperature of the meat.

THE BEAST WITHIN

Stuffing one bird or beast inside of another is nothing new. The ancient Romans did it, and so did the medieval French. The British fell in line and someone carried the concept to the Americas. Whether it is the classic Cajun turducken you crave or some other modern mythical megabeast, we implore you to think this one through before you begin. Although we are certainly not purists and we do adore a meaty project, the beast within the beast seems like a bust. A large part of the joy of a roast, stuffed or otherwise, is the juxtaposition of crispy, brown exterior and moist, juicy interior. If a chicken and a duck are stuffed into a turkey, they are essentially steamed while the turkey roasts, which does keep the whole project moist but severely diminishes the ratio of crispy skin to moist meat. That is a trade-off we cannot endorse.

How to Truss a Bird for Roasting

Trussing chicken yields a extra regular and compact shape, which enables the fowl to prepare dinner dinner extra calmly and stops the portions that protrude from the frame, along with the legs and wings, from drying out at some stage in roasting.

1. Season the fowl thoroughly, inner and out, then position, breast facet up, on a piece

surface. Fold the wing guidelines in the back of the fowl's back.

2. Cut a chunk of butcher's cord as a minimum four feet (1.2 m) long. Place the center of the cord in the back of the neck of the fowl, then circle every cease of the cord one complete rotation across the wing joint on both facet. Pull every cease of the cord tightly withinside the course of the legs, so as to press the lowest of the wings without delay in opposition to the frame of the fowl.

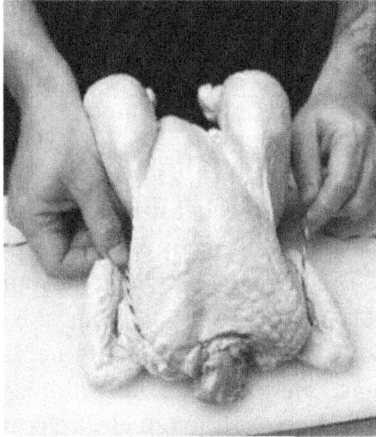

3. Place the cord withinside the groove among the leg and the frame, then pass the cord without delay below the lowest of the breastbone, pulling it tight as you'll a shoelace.

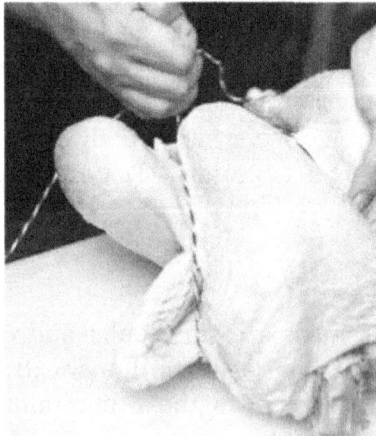

4. Cross the legs of the fowl and convey the ends of the cord round the lowest of every leg to tie the legs together. Circle the legs as soon as with the cord, then

make stronger this tie with a knot.

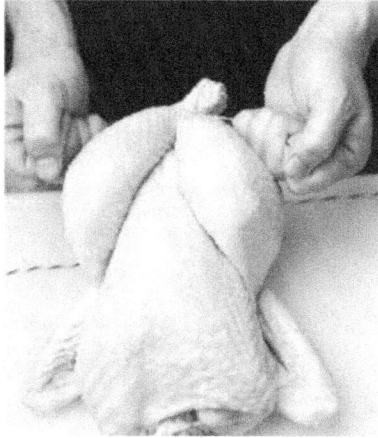

5. Clip any greater cord away, and voilà! You have a trussed oven-geared up fowl.

Fig-and-Sausage Stuffed Quail

FIG-AND-SAUSAGE STUFFED QUAIL

We want to get our fill of clean figs at some stage in their short season in past due summer. Roasted figs have an particularly rich, honeyed taste that may be a excellent fit for each chicken and beef. This crammed quail manages to marry all three: an entire ripe fig is encased in an egg-fashioned ball of beef sausage, that is then crammed into the hollow space of a brined quail. As the quail roasts, the

sausage enables to maintain the little fowl wet and the recent fig exudes its candy juices into the meat.

SERVES FOUR
eight cups (2 L) boiling water
4.6 ounces (one hundred thirty g) high-quality sea salt
three.eight ounces (108 g) sugar
four semiboneless (glove-boned) quail
12 ounces (340 g) Lemon and Herb Pork Sausage
four small-to-medium figs
1 tablespoon rendered duck fats or unsalted butter, melted

To make the brine, pour the boiling water right into a massive heatproof box or bowl. (Be certain to degree the water after it has come to a boil, as a few will evaporate because it heats and measuring in advance will bring about overly salty brine). Add the salt and sugar and stir to dissolve.

Let cool for numerous mins then refrigerate the brine till cold.

When the brine has cooled to 50°F (10°C), cast off from the fridge and upload the quail. Make certain they're completely submerged, topping them with a plate if necessary. Cover the box, go back it to the fridge, and go away the birds to brine for three hours.

Meanwhile, collect the fig-filled sausage balls. Divide the sausage into 4 three-ounce (eighty five g) portions. Shape every component right into a patty approximately ½ inch (12 mm) thick. Trim the stem off of every fig. Place a fig, stemmed facet down, without delay at the middle of a sausage patty. Bring the sausage up across the fig, urgent it towards the fig and maintaining the stemmed facet withinside the middle. Mold the sausage across the fig right into a tough egg shape, with a narrower pinnacle and a much wider base. Repeat with the ultimate figs and sausage patties.

Preheat the oven to 425°F (220°C). Outfit a roasting pan with a rack. Remove the quail from the brine, draining them nicely after which patting them dry. Gently pry aside the legs of a quail and stuff a sausage ball, slender quit first, into the cavity. Once the ball is snugly in the quail, pass the bird's legs and tie them collectively with a 6inch (15 cm) duration of butcher's cord. Repeat with the ultimate balls and quail.

Brush the quail on all aspects with the duck fats and vicinity them, breast facet up, at the rack, spacing them as a minimum 2 inches (five cm) aside. Place the pan withinside the oven and roast for 22 to 24 minutes, till a thermometer inserted without delay into the center of the stuffing registers 140°F (60°C).

Remove the quail from the oven and allow relaxation for five minutes, then snip the cord and serve.

Pork Shoulder Pot Roast Stuffed with Garlic, Greens, and Walnuts

PORK SHOULDER POT ROAST STUFFED WITH

GARLIC, GREENS, AND WALNUTS

Chock-complete of greens, this easy beef shoulder pot roast, made with Boston butt, makes a nourishing and comforting supper. Abundant, leafy Swiss chard has a tendency to be to be had year-spherical and is the usual for this stuffing, however it's miles similarly suitable made with spinach, mustard, kale, or different seasonal greens.

SERVES EIGHT TO 10
I entire boneless, skinless beef Boston butt, approximately eight pounds (three.6 kg)
Fine sea salt and freshly floor pepper
three bunches Swiss chard or different leafy greens, stemmed 10 cloves garlic, sliced paper-thin
¾ cup (eighty five g) chopped toasted walnuts
I ½ cups (360 ml) beef, chicken, or duck broth (see Basic Rich Broth)
I ½ cups (360 ml) cups dry pink wine

One day earlier of cooking, season and equipped the roast for stuffing. First, make the pocket for the stuffing with the aid of using creating a horizontal reduce thru the center of the roast, following the seam wherein the bone changed into removed. Leave one of the 4 edges absolutely intact. Open the roast like a ee-e book. Season liberally on each aspects with salt and pepper. Close the ee-e book, wrap tightly with plastic wrap, and refrigerate overnight.

Remove the roast from the fridge and permit it to mood for two hours. Preheat the oven to 350°F (180°C).

Bring a massive pot of salted water to a rolling boil. Add the chard leaves and blanch for approximately 2 minutes. Drain and allow cool, then squeeze out any extra water. Chop the chard coarsely.

Open the beef shoulder like a ee-e book, with the intact side for your left. Arrange the chard withinside the middle of the roast in a neat layer, leaving a 1-inch (2.five cm) border exposed surrounding it. Distribute the garlic frivolously over the chard, observed with the aid of using the walnuts. Fold the pinnacle a part of the roast over the stuffing and tie tightly with butcher's cord in 3 places, spacing the loops frivolously and reinforcing the ee-e book shape.

Outfit a massive braiser with a rack. Place the beef shoulder, fatty facet going through up, at the rack. (If you don't have a rack that suits your pot, halve some leeks lengthwise, vicinity them on the lowest of the pot, and placed the roast at the leeks; they'll assist the roast well at some point of cooking.)

Transfer the pot to the oven and roast for approximately forty five minutes. Remove the pot from the oven and thoroughly pour off the rendered fats. Reserve those pan drippings for some other use. Add the broth and wine to the pot and go back it to the oven. Turn down the oven temperature to 300°F (150°C) and hold to cook, basting the roast each 30 minutes, for approximately 2½ hours. The roast is prepared whilst it's miles a wealthy golden brown, fork-tender, and a chunk wobbly.

Transfer the roast to a slicing board and allow it relaxation for 20 minutes. Snip the cord and reduce the roast into thick slices. Bathe every serving with a spoonful of the cooking juices.

Wild Mushroom–Stuffed Pork Rib Roast

WILD MUSHROOM–STUFFED PORK RIB ROAST

Versatile mushroom duxelles makes an outstanding and splendidly earthy stuffing for beef, raising an regular rib roast to special-event status. The duxelles flavors the beef and gives moisture for the tilt muscle meat because it roasts, maintaining it juicy and delicious. The addition of wobbly gelée to the duxelles offers the stuffing structure, binding it in order that

while it comes time to carve and serve, every slice has a

fetching eye of untamed mushroom.

SERVES FOUR TO 6
five-rib beef loin rack with chine bone removed, ideally from the shoulder end
Fine sea salt and freshly floor pepper
1½ cups (244 g) Wild Mushroom Duxelles

One day ahead, butterfly, season, and stuff the roast. First, stand the rack on a slicing board in order that the ribs factor upward and towards the right (towards the left in case you are a southpaw). Make an incision alongside the pinnacle of the roast immediately in the back of the ribs, urgent into the bone. Grip the unfastened strip of meat that consequences from this reduce and peel the beef farfar from the bone as you carve towards the ribs, to open the roast like a book.

Season the roast liberally on each aspects with salt and pepper. Stuff the duxelles into the pocket, leaving a 1-inch (2.five cm) border exposed on all aspects. Gently near the roast returned up into its unique shape, taking care now no longer to displace the mushrooms. To tie the roast, lay it fats aspect down in your board and run a period of cord below it parallel to the ribs. Tie a butcher's knot (see How to Tie a Roast) among the primary ribs of the rack. Repeat this knot among every rib to complete trussing, then wrap the roast in plastic wrap and refrigerate overnight.

Remove the roast from the fridge and mood it for approximately 30 minutes. Preheat the oven to 375°F (190°C). Outfit a roasting pan with a rack.

Place the roast, fats aspect up, at the rack. Place the pan withinside the oven and roast for 30 to forty minutes, till the fats has caramelized and became a deep golden brown. Turn down the oven temperature to 300°F (150°C) and hold to prepare dinner dinner for every other 30 to forty minutes, till a thermometer inserted into the thickest a part of the loin registers 140°F (60°C).

Remove the roast from the oven and permit relaxation for 20 minutes. Snip the cord and reduce among the ribs to serve.

DUCK STUFFED WITH FARRO, FIGS, AND HAZELNUTS

Golden, crispy roast duck is a festive centerpiece for a celebratory meal, in particular while full of sage-scented sausage, purple wine–soaked figs, toasted hazelnuts, and farro. *Farro, an historic varietal of wheat famous in valuable Italy, is*

a fave withinside the Fatted Calf kitchen, wherein we upload it to hearty soups and rustic salads. When cooked, it has a company however chewy texture that still makes it best to be used in stuffings. Although we just like the toasty, nutty taste of farro in aggregate with duck, this stuffing works similarly properly with quail, recreation hens, or different birds.

SERVES 6

1 ½ cups (360 ml) dry purple wine 2 tablespoons sugar

1 dried bay leaf

1 sprig thyme, plus 2 tablespoons chopped sparkling thyme

½ teaspoon peppercorns

1 allspice berry

Fine sea salt and freshly floor pepper

12 dried figs

1 entire duck, five to 7 pounds (2.three to three.2 kg)

1 pound (450 g) Breakfast Sausage

2 cups (330 g) cooked farro or wild rice

¾ cup (a hundred g) hazelnuts, toasted, skinned, and coarsely chopped

¼ cup (15 g) chopped sparkling flat-leaf parsley

One day in advance, put together the figs. In a small saucepan, stir collectively the purple wine, sugar, bay leaf, thyme sprig, peppercorns, allspice, and a pinch of salt. Bring to a simmer over excessive warmth to dissolve the sugar and permit the taste of the spices to bloom. Remove from the warmth and pour over the figs. Cover and refrigerate overnight. Bone the duck, following the commands for a Whole Boned Bird, going across the legs and wings and ensuring you do now no longer make any holes withinside the skin. Work cautiously across the breastbone, leaving the tenders connected to the breast. Trim any glands or blood vessels off of the beef as soon as it's far absolutely off the bone. Season the duck internal and out with salt and pepper.

Preheat the oven to 375°F (190°C). Outfit a roasting pan with a rack.

To make the stuffing, first drain the figs. Cut off the stem of every fig, then region the figs lengthwise. In a bowl, integrate the sausage, *farro*, figs, hazelnuts, chopped thyme, and parsley. Pat the stuffing right into a cylinder approximately three inches (7.five cm) in diameter and three inches (7.five cm) shorter than the duck. Lay the stuffing immediately at the center of the duck and roll the beef tightly across the stuffing. Lightly rating the pores and skin in a crosshatch sample to facilitate the discharge of fats throughout cooking. Truss the duck tightly (see How to Tie a Roast).

Place the duck at the rack and region the pan withinside the oven. Roast the duck, basting it after the primary 20 mins with the drippings which have collected withinside the pan, for approximately 1 hour or till a thermometer inserted into the center of the stuffing registers 140°F (60°C). If the pores and skin begins offevolved to get a touch too brown, you may decrease the oven temperature to 325°F (165°C) so the duck finishes greater slowly.

Remove the duck from the oven and allow relaxation for 10 mins. Carve into slices 1 inch (2.five cm) thick to serve.

SAUSAGE, SALAMI & THEIR COUSINS

Make sausage. Make sausage to reclaim the candy recollections of supper at nonna's, smoky outdoor barbecues, and sunny baseball games. Make sausage to revel in all over again the unabashed pleasure of tasting a plump Oktoberfest wurst. Make sausage to embark at the quest to seize the essence of an pleasing lemongrass heady fragrance wafting withinside the air of a crowded night time market. Grind, stuff, and hyperlink sausage with pals and with own circle of relatives to find out wherein your meals comes from and to comprehend the exertions that brings it on your table. Make sausage and create some thing from almost not anything the manner our ancestors have achieved for lots of years.

Sausage making is a craft born of necessity, a manner to make the maximum of the bizarre bits, scraps of meat, blood, fats, and entrails. At the maximum simple level, sausage is simply pro floor meat. The components and seasonings you operate and the manner the beef is ready are what make every sausage unique.

Making your very own sausage is a worthwhile challenge that want now no longer be complicated. If you're simply beginning to learn how to make your very own sausage, start with the simple sausages and their versions beginning here. The techniques for making easy sparkling sausages are the premise for generating all forms of sausage and salami. As you grow to be greater adept at marinating, grinding, and mixing, you may attempt your hand at casing sparkling sausage. Once you've got got practiced the numerous casing techniques, you may be capable of crank out hyperlinks and loops to put together poached or smoked sausages, and in case you need to head a step further, you may even evidently ferment your sausages to make salami.

The Sausage Shop

Although making sausage isn't complicated, it does require area, time, gear, and a touch forethought. Preparation is key. You will want to installation your very own sausage save or workspace, accumulate all the critical gear and components, and feature a radical know-how of any recipe earlier than you get cranking.

Workspace

You want lots of room to cut, grind, and case meat. Choose a piece place that provides a touch elbow room, geared up with a piece floor that may be a cushty peak for you. Keep it freed from inessentials. Have handiest the gear you want and a stack of smooth kitchen towels. For smooth access, lay your gear out a baking sheet or tray coated with a smooth towel earlier than you start. If your stop intention is a smoked sausage, dried sausage, or salami, you may need to have equipped a area to grasp your completed sausage (see Hanging Salami for Initial Fermentation and for Drying).

Time

Sausage takes time. Simple, uncased sparkling sausages would possibly take handiest an hour to assemble, however as you development to cased and cooked sausages or dried sausage and salami, the procedure can take some days. It's a very good concept to interrupt up the challenge into steps and unfold the stairs out over numerous days, instead of attempt to perform an excessive amount of too quickly, specially whilst you have become the grasp of it. Plan to accumulate your substances an afternoon or ahead. Seasoning or marinating the beef is fine achieved the day earlier than, even though hours will suffice in case you are pressed for time. If you're making ready a cooked sausage, you should permit a further day to grasp the sparkling sausage earlier than you poach or smoke it.

Tools of the Trade

Although you could make easy uncased sausage with freshly floor meat from a butcher shop, spices, and your very own arms, we inspire you to make the leap and attempt your hand at grinding your very own meat and casing your sausage. This calls for a touch funding in a few top tools. If you're simply starting to make sausage, begin easy and be practical approximately what you truely want. You can usually red meat up your series as you hone your craft.

Meat Grinders

Manual Grinders: This is your grandma's grinder. It normally clamps to a table. You feed the cubes of meat into the hopper, flip the crank, and out comes freshly floor meat. This is extraordinary in case you need to grind a noticeably small amount of meat for sausage patties, burgers, or meatballs. It's small and smooth to assemble, clean, and store. But for grinding extra than more than one kilos of meat, you can locate it too time-consuming. Also, those old school grinders paintings properly best if the blade is sharpened or changed regularly.

Electric Multipurpose: If you already very own a stand mixer, you could get a grinder attachment this is compact, smooth to use, smooth to clean, and low-priced. The disadvantage is that those machines lack chutzpah. The blade and grinder plates aren't as long lasting and powerful as the ones on a bigger system. That means, to grind approximately five kilos (2.three kg) of meat, you'll want to permit approximately 10 minutes. But in case you are simply starting or in case you best make sausage some instances a yr and in small quantities, this kind of system gets the process done.

Electric Single Purpose: If you're a gearhead, a devoted sausage fanatic, or seeking to upgrade, you'll need a stand-on my own grinder. You'll locate many one-of-a-kind fashions of single-purpose, tabletop electric powered grinders at the market, and maximum of them will do the process properly. Look for a system that has electric desires well suited with the voltage to be had on your workspace and elements which might be without difficulty replaceable. See Sources for grinder retailers.

Clockwise from pinnacle left: stomper, collar, knife, plate, worm, feeder tube

Sausage Stuffers

Electric: If you already very own a stand mixer with a grinder attachment, you could get a totally low-priced stuffer attachment this is compact and smooth to use. Many guide and electric powered grinders additionally have optionally available stuffer attachments. The disadvantage of a stuffer connected to a grinder is that the beef should byskip thru the mechanism a 2nd time earlier than it is going right into a casing, that can negatively have an effect on the feel by mashing the beef. However, if area and charge are an issue, that is truely an option.

Hand Crank: If you experience making sausage, a hand-crank stuffer is really well worth the funding. All of them perform at the identical premise. They are made from a base, a canister or cylinder wherein you load the freshly floor sausage, and a crank or deal with which you rotate to transport the gears that manipulate the piston that presses the sausage thru the nozzle. Nozzles of various sizes paintings with diverse casings to provide sausages of various diameters.

When searching for a hand-crank sausage stuffer, you've got got the selection among horizontal and vertical designs. Horizontal stuffers, even though regularly attractive, aren't in particular practical. The layout calls for that they be located at the brink of a worktable, they regularly require units of arms to characteristic properly, and that they absorb a large amount of area. Vertical stuffers are the extra not unusualplace and flexible choice. A vertical stuffer calls for best one user, has a crank positioned on the pinnacle of the system that lets in you to place it everywhere at the paintings floor, and takes up no less than floor area.

Smokehouses

Smokehouses may be constructed from sincerely anything, from vintage oil drums and family chimneys to cinder blocks and plywood. If cash isn't anyt any object, deluxe fashions are to be had for purchase, with temperature controls and virtual displays. Most are larger than a bread box, however a few are the dimensions of a walk-in closet. If you're handiest making plans to smoke one batch of sausages at a time, then you may escape with a smaller, bread-box-length model. When identifying what form of smokehouse is proper for you, supply your self an sincere appraisal of your DIY constructing talents and recollect how often you may be the usage of it, whether or not you may be the usage of it to bloodless smoke, warm smoke, or each, how plenty you may be smoking at any given time, and what kind of room you need to keep your smokehouse. There is a dialogue of smokehouses in Chapter 7, so in case you're making plans to make any of the smoked sausage recipes on this chapter, examine approximately Finishing with Smoke.

Sausage Knife

A sausage knife has a small, sharp paring blade on one stop and tines on the alternative stop. It is a available device used at some point of the stuffing process. The knife stop is used to reduce casings and twine, and the tines are used to pierce the crammed casing to launch air bubbles.

S Hooks

S hooks of numerous styles and sizes are indispensable. Larger S hooks (6 to eight inches/15 to twenty cm) are extraordinary for putting lengths of sausages to set in a single day or withinside the smokehouse. Smaller S hooks (approximately 1 inch/2.five cm) are available for putting character salami for lengthy durations of time.

Scales

Most recipes for sausage offer measurements in weight. Not handiest is meat normally bought via way of means of weight however a weight dimension is likewise normally greater correct than a extent dimension. A small virtual digital scale that measures in increments of .01 kilos or kilograms will offer you with the maximum correct results.

Alternatively, in case you need some thing a touch greater vintage school, a sturdy, calibrated analog platform scale with a potential of as a minimum 10 kilos (or five kg) will do the trick.

Ingredients: Meat and Fat

All sausage is comprised especially of meat and fats, normally in a ratio of approximately 25 percentage fats to seventy five percentage lean meat. When you store for meat to make sausage, pick out fattier or untrimmed cuts, in order to offer you with a chunk of each meat and fats.

Poultry and Rabbit

You can use almost any form of fowl to make sausage. If you're the usage of entire birds, larger or greater mature ones are higher. Look for fowl labeled "stewer." The meat to bone ratio has a tendency to be better in a bigger bird, and the muscle groups have had time to emerge as greater absolutely evolved, yielding greater flavorful results. If you've got got the choice of the usage of fowl parts, choose breasts over legs and thighs, that have tendons on the way to want to be removed.

Larger or stewer rabbits are most effective for the identical reasons. Except for the bony forelegs, you may use nearly each a part of the rabbit, which include the hind legs, saddle, skirt, tenders, and kidneys. Even the liver may be floor in with the beef or diced and folded into the farce.

Both fowl and rabbit are pretty lean and require extra fats to make sausage. Using fowl fats to provide an all-fowl sausage isn't always recommended, however. Poultry fats is at risk of smearing at some point of grinding and liquefies conveniently at some point of cooking, leaving you with a dry and unappetizing sausage. Most commercially produced fowl sausage incorporates stabilizers including collagen or gelatin to counteract smearing. Adding a touch beef again fats is a herbal opportunity that works nicely.

Pork

The pig turned into almost designed for sausage making, and beef makes the maximum reliably scrumptious sausage. Good-great beef is flavorful on its own, but it is able to additionally play a great assisting position for a whole lot of different flavors.

Buy meat from a totally grown hog (it need to be over one hundred fifty kilos/sixty eight kg). Mature hogs with well-evolved muscle groups and a great fats content material are favored over younger, leaner pigs, that are higher acceptable to roasting. The herbal fats content material of a boneless Boston butt is normally perfect for sausage making, however you may additionally use a combination of lean and fats trimmings from different cuts of beef, so long as the fats content material is ready 25 percentage. If you're the usage of extra beef fats, tougher again fats is top-rated to the softer leg and stomach fats.

Lamb

Lamb sausage has a exceptional taste that stands as much as excessive spicing or strong, herbaceous seasonings. Boneless shoulder, shank, neck, and leg are all extraordinary cuts for sausage making. If needed, extra fats may be taken from the breast or shoulder.

Lamb fats may be very corporation and desires to be floor twice. It also can be strongly flavored. If you're making an all-lamb sausage, do not forget substituting olive oil for a part of the fats or creating a sausage with a fats content material barely decrease than the conventional 25 percent. Alternatively, in case you have a tendency to shrink back from the more potent taste of lamb, strive the usage of 1/2 of red meat and 1/2 of lamb to your recipe, for a sausage with a subtler lamb taste and the high-quality texture of red meat.

Beef

Beef has an earthy flavor, and beef sausages tend to be highly spiced. Chuck, brisket, sirloin, and trimmings from roasts (such as the side muscle off of the tenderloin) make excellent sausage. Brisket and chuck are usually at least 25 percent fat, so no additional fat is needed. If possible, request untrimmed beef cuts from your butcher. If you are using leaner cuts and need additional fat, the rib-eye fat cap works well. Beef fat is firm, so always grind it twice. Avoid suet (kidney fat), as it is too soft for sausage making.

BASIC RECIPES FOR SAUSAGE
POULTRY OR RABBIT

3¾ pounds (1.7 kg) boneless, skinless hen or rabbit
+ 1¼ pound (567 g) red meat again fats
+ 2 tablespoons (1.2 ounces/34 g) pleasant sea salt
—

five pounds (2.three kg) simple hen or rabbit sausage

LAMB
three pounds (1.four kg) boneless lamb shoulder
+ 2 pounds (900 g) lean boneless lamb foreshank or
  hind shank
+ 2 tablespoons (1.2 ounces/34 g) sea salt
+ 2 tablespoons olive oil
—

five pounds (2.three kg) simple all-lamb sausage

Alternatively

2½ pounds (1.2 kg) boneless lamb shoulder
+ 2½ pounds (1.2 kg) boneless red meat picnic
+ 2 tablespoons (1.2 ounces/34 g) sea salt
—

five pounds (2.three kg) simple lamb and red meat sausage

PORK
4½ pounds (2 kg) boneless red meat picnic

+ eight ounces (225 g) red meat again fats or

five pounds (2.three kg) boneless red meat Boston butt
+ 2 tablespoons (1.2 ounces/34 g) pleasant sea salt
—

five pounds (2.three kg) simple red meat sausage

BEEF
five pounds (2.three kg) untrimmed red meat chuck or brisket
+ 2 tablespoons (1.2 ounces/34 g) sea salt
—

five pounds (2.three kg) simple all-red meat sausage

Alternatively

three pounds (1.four kg) untrimmed red meat which
includes chuck or brisket
+ 2 pounds (900 g) red meat Boston butt
+ 2 tablespoons (1.2 ounces/34 g) sea salt
—
five pounds (2.three kg) simple red meat and red meat
sausage

Basic Sausage Method

The technique for making almost each type of sausage starts with the identical steps. First, you bring together a spice package and reduce the beef. Next, you blend the beef with the spices, depart it to marinate for a while, after which grind it. Once it's far floor, the beef is blended once more through hand. The sausage is now equipped to apply or equipped to case.

Step 1: Assemble the Spice Kit

Your spice package includes the elements you may be the usage of to taste your sausage. Many sausage-making deliver groups promote readymade spice kits, however toasting and grinding your very own spices makes a distinction you may taste.

Begin through measuring the salt. Then degree your spices. If the recipe requires toasted spices, you may need to toast them in a 325°F (165°C) oven for three to five minutes. Allow them to cool, then grind them collectively in a spice grinder. For maximum sausage, except in any other case indicated, you may need to grind your spices very finely. Mix the floor spices with the salt. If the recipe requires garlic, mince it finely after which upload it to the spice package along side any complete spices.

Step 2: Cutting

Cut the beef into especially uniform cubes which might be smaller than the outlet of your grinder (for maximum grinders, 1-inch/2.five cm cubes are best). Remove any blood vessels, tendons, or glands. Place the cubed meat in a nonreactive bowl or box massive sufficient to permit room for mixing.

Step 3: Marinating

Evenly distribute 1/2 of of the contents of the spice package over the beef. Using your fingers blend the beef properly till calmly coated. Add the second one 1/2 of of the package and blend once more. Cover and refrigerate for at the least 12 hours or for up to two days to permit the seasonings to permeate the beef.

Step 4: Chilling

Sausage loves to be stored bloodless. Chilling each your meat and elements of the grinder facilitates to keep away from grinding problems which includes smearing. Keeping the beef bloodless earlier than and at some stage in the technique additionally extends the shelf existence of the completed sausage. After slicing and marinating the beef, make certain to refrigerate it for at the least 2 hours and ideally overnight, in order that it's far very well chilled. You also can refrigerate the elements of the grinder. Keep the whole thing refrigerated till you're equipped to grind.

Step 5: Grinding

Whichever kind of grinder you use, the mechanics and setup are basically the identical. Begin through attaching the feeder tube to the bottom of the machine. Insert the worm (see photo) into the tube. Attach the blade or knife, flat facet out, to the worm. Most grinders include more than one plates to let you range the scale of the grind. Choose the plate for the kind of grind you are attempting to achieve. Attach the plate flush with the outlet of the feeder tube. Screw the collar onto the give up of the tube securely, however do now no longer overtighten. If your grinder is prepared with a tray, connect it to the pinnacle of the feeder tube.

You will want a extensive nonreactive bowl or box that suits effortlessly beneathneath the grinder to capture the floor meat. Remove the beef from the refrigerator. If you're the use of an electric powered grinder flip it on. Feed the beef into the tube, one piece at a time. Let the device do the paintings in preference to push an excessive amount of meat via the grinder at once. If you're the use of an electric powered grinder, permit the device to run for a complete minute after the remaining of the beef has been fed via the tube to expel any remnants. Wipe the face of the plate smooth at the same time as the device continues to be walking after which flip the device off. In maximum cases, you'll grind a batch of meat handiest once.

The exceptions are burger meat, pork fats, lamb fats, and sausages with a totally clean consistency, which want to be floor twice.

Step 6: Mixing

Seasoned, floor sausage meat, additionally called the farce or forcemeat, desires to be blended very well through hand for 1 to two minutes. This action, much like kneading bread dough, enables to increase the proteins that bind the sausage together. It additionally guarantees that the seasonings are flippantly dispensed throughout. When a extra homogenous texture is desired, a few sausage meat is blended similarly in a stand mixer geared up with the paddle attachment or in a meals processor. This method is referred to as emulsifying.

Step 7: Tasting

Scoop up about 2 tablespoons of the well-mixed farce and shape into a small, flat patty. Cook the patty in a small pan over medium heat. Evaluate the taste and texture. If the sausage seems dry and crumbly, incorporate a small amount of ground fat. If the seasoning needs to be more pronounced, add more salt or spices. If the sausage is too highly seasoned for your taste, add a small amount of unseasoned ground meat and ground fat to help to absorb some of the excess. Remember, it is much easier to add salt and spices than it is to lessen their intensity once the farce is prepared. If you tend to like mildly seasoned sausage, start with about half the amount of salt and spices and add more to taste if needed.

SMEARING

If the fats starts to squeeze out of the perimeters of the grinder in shiny, flat ribbons or via the die in greasy-searching streaks, stop! You have smearing, a circumstance which can damage the feel of your sausage. You want to halt grinding, discover the cause, and treatment the situation. Here are 3 number one reasons and their solutions:

1. The grinder or the beef is simply too warm. Check

thetemperature of the beef and the grinder. Wash the grinder, kick back down the grinder components and any unground meat for 30 minutes, and begin over.

2. The knife is inserted backward. Take aside thegrinder. Wash and kick back the components and reassemble carefully, ensuring the knife is dealing with flat aspect out.

3. The knife blade is dull. Knife blades do put on out over time. Keeping a spare blade on hand is always a good idea. Replace the blade and make sure to have the old blade sharpened.

THE UGLY BURGER

A burger is basically a totally fundamental pork sausage. Of course, now that we've confused the significance of marinating and mixing, overlook all of that. The guiding precept in the back of The Ugly Burger is to season the beef simply earlier than cooking and to control it as low as viable for a homely however fantastically tender, juicy burger so that it will depart you questioning how some thing so unpleasant and easy may want to likely flavor so good.

**MAKES FOUR 8-OUNCE
(225 G) BURGERS**
1 pound (450 g) boneless pork chuck, reduce into 1-inch (2.five cm) cubes
1 pound (450 g) boneless pork quick rib, cutinto 1-inch (2.five cm) cubes
2 teaspoons pleasant sea salt

Place all the pork right into a nonreactive bowl and refrigerate for 1 hour. Refrigerate the components of your grinder till prepared to use.

Prepare a warm hearthplace for direct-warmth grilling in a charcoal grill.

Assemble the grinder with the medium plate and grind the chilled pork once. Sprinkle 1/2 of of the salt over the floor pork, after which grind again. Without mixing, divide the floor meat into four identical portions. Carefully flatten every component in a patty 1 inch (2.five cm) thick and lightly spherical the edges. A few cracks are okay. Make a small indentation withinside the center of every patty together along with your thumb to maintain the burger from contracting for the duration of cooking, then sprinkle the closing salt over each sides.

Place the patties at the grill grate at once over the coals and grill, turning frequently, for approximately four to six minutes, or till finished in your liking.

Duck and Lemongrass Sausage Patties

DUCK AND LEMONGRASS SAUSAGE PATTIES

These aromatic sausage patties are splendid grilled and utilized in a easy rice-bowl meal with herbs or in a banh mi (Vietnamese sandwich). The aggregate also can be crumbled right into a stir-fry, grilled on skewers (or lemongrass, as withinside the photo), encased in a dumpling wrapper and steamed, or shaped into little meatballs and mixed with noodles in a noodle soup broth.

MAKES EIGHT FIVE-OUNCE (A HUNDRED AND FORTY G) PATTIES

1 pound, 14 ounces (850 g) boneless, skinless duck meat, reduce into 1-inch (2.five cm) cubes
10 ounces (280 g) red meat returned fats, reduce into 1inch (2.five cm) cubes 1 tablespoon (6 ounces/17 g) pleasant sea salt
2 teaspoons freshly floor pepper 1 teaspoon sugar
2 teaspoons fish sauce
1 tablespoon minced shallot
1 tablespoon minced lemongrass
1½ teaspoons peeled, grated, then chopped clean ginger
1½ teaspoons minced garlic

Place the duck and fats in a nonreactive bowl or container. To make the spice package, integrate the salt, pepper, sugar, fish sauce, shallot, lemongrass, ginger, and garlic and blend nicely. Mix the spice package frivolously with the beef (see Basic Sausage Method), cover, and refrigerate in a single day.

Refrigerate the elements of your grinder till equipped to use. Following the commands for grinding, match the grinder with smallest plate and grind the beef once. Mix the farce nicely via way of means of hand for two minutes. Cook a small pattern of the aggregate in a sauté pan and modify the seasonings if necessary. For patties, divide the farce into four same quantities and punctiliously flatten every component right into a patty ¾ inch (2 cm) thick. Grill, crumble, or in any other case revel in as cautioned withinside the headnote.

LAMB AND HERB MEATBALLS

Aleppo pepper, named for the Silk Road metropolis of Aleppo, in Syria, is famous at some stage in the Middle East, the Mediterranean, and in our kitchen on the Fatted Calf, wherein it makes an look in severa recipes, which include lots of our favourite lamb dishes. The vibrant, flaky floor chile has a sharp, nearly citrus-flavored sting this is accompanied via way of means of a mellow, earthy contemporary of heat, a best that stays awesome even withinside the landscape of herbs and spices used to season those savory meatballs.

These meatballs may be browned in olive oil after which simmered in Chile Tomato Sauce or skewered and grilled. Alternatively, to make lamb burgers, divide the farce into 6 same quantities and form every component right into a patty ¾ inch (2 cm) thick.

MAKES ABOUT 36 SMALL MEATBALLS
I teaspoon fenugreek seeds
I teaspoon black peppercorns
I teaspoon coriander seeds
I teaspoon yellow mustard seeds
I big allspice berry
I small dried bay leaf
I tablespoon high-quality sea salt
I ½ teaspoons overwhelmed dried Aleppo
pepper 2 teaspoons finely chopped garlic
2½ pounds (1.2 kg) boneless lamb shoulder or leg, reduce into
I- inch (2.five cm) cubes
I tablespoon grated yellow onion
2 tablespoons chopped clean
mint
2 tablespoons chopped clean cilantro
¼ cup (15 g) chopped clean flat-leaf parsley
I tablespoon olive oil

Preheat the oven to 325°F (165°C). Spread the fenugreek, black peppercorns, coriander, mustard, and allspice on a baking sheet and toast for three to five minutes, till fragrant. Let cool completely, then switch to a spice grinder, upload the bay, and grind finely.

To make the spice package, in a small bowl, integrate the freshly floor spices, salt, Aleppo pepper, and garlic and blend nicely. Place the lamb in a nonreactive bowl or container. Mix the spice package frivolously with the beef (see Basic Sausage Method), cover, and refrigerate in a single day.

Refrigerate the elements of your grinder till equipped to use.

Following the commands for grinding, match the grinder with the smallest plate and grind the beef twice. Add the onion, mint, cilantro, parsley, and olive oil and blend nicely via way of means of hand for two to a few minutes. The aggregate need to start to corporation up and experience cohesive. Cook a small pattern of the aggregate in a sauté pan and modify the seasonings if necessary. Roll the aggregate into meatballs approximately 1½ inches (four cm) in diameter, then use in one of the scrumptious methods designated withinside the headnote.

OAXACAN-STYLE CHORIZO

This is a boldly pro chorizo we advanced for our buddies at Rancho Gordo, in Napa, California, after they have been hosting

esteemed Mexican-meals author Diana Kennedy. In addition to promoting a extensive type of dried beans, chiles, grains, and different meals products, Rancho Gordo consists of an intensely tropical banana vincgar that gives a fruity counterpoint for the earthy, fiery chiles.

We typically depart this chorizo unfastened to be used in little tacos, for blending with potatoes, or for including to soups and stews. It also can be positioned into red meat casings approximately a foot (30 cm) long, tied into loops, hung in a single day in a groovy place, after which grilled slowly or smoked.

MAKES A GENEROUS FIVE POUNDS (2.THREE KG)
four pounds (1.eight kg) boneless red meat picnic, reduce into
1-inch (2.five cm) cubes
1 pound (450 g) red meat lower back fats, reduce into 1inch
(2.five cm) cubes 2 tablespoons plus 1 teaspoon (1.four
ounces/
forty g) high-
quality sea salt 6
guajillo chiles
6 ancho chiles
2 morita chipotle chiles
three dried árbol chiles
2 teaspoons peppercorns
6 allspice berries
2 tablespoons cumin seeds
four entire cloves
1½-inch (four cm) piece cinnamon
stick five cloves garlic, unpeeled
½ cup fruity vinegar (including banana, pineapple, or
cider) 1 teaspoon achiote powder
2 tablespoons chopped sparkling
thyme 2 tablespoons chopped
sparkling oregano

Place the beef and fats in a massive nonreactive bowl. Season the beef with the salt. Cover and refrigerate overnight.

Toast all the chiles on a comal (a Mexican griddle) or a solid iron frying pan over medium warmness for approximately 1 minute, till aromatic and pliable. Turn out onto a plate to cool. Remove the stem and seeds from every chile and discard. Tear the chiles into smaller pieces, vicinity in a bowl, upload heat water to cover, and permit soak for approximately 30 minutes, till softened. Drain the chiles, booking the chiles and some tablespoons of the soaking liquid separately.

Using the equal comal or frying pan, toast the peppercorns,

allspice, cumin, cloves, and cinnamon stick over medium warmness for two to a few minutes, till aromatic. Let cool to room temperature, then switch to a spice grinder and grind finely.

Dry roast the garlic at the equal comal or frying pan over medium warmness for approximately five minutes, till the pores and skin darkens and the garlic releases a aromatic aroma. When the cloves are cool sufficient to handle, peel and chop.

In a blender, integrate the vinegar, chiles, floor spices, garlic, and achiote powder and puree till smooth. If the aggregate is simply too thick, skinny with reserved chile soaking liquid as had to attain an excellent consistency. Scrape the puree right into a massive nonreactive bowl and fold withinside the thyme and oregano. Place the bowl immediately beneathneath the beef grinder.

Refrigerate the components of your grinder till prepared to use. Following the commands for grinding, in shape the grinder with the most important plate and grind the beef as soon as immediately into the chile-spice puree. Mix the farce nicely through hand for two to a few minutes. The aggregate must start to organization up and sense cohesive. Cook a small pattern of the aggregate in a sauté pan and modify the seasonings if necessary. Use as counseled withinside the headnote.

SAUSAGE AND SEASONING CHART

You can use the fundamental sausage recipes to create a number of distinctive sausages through changing the spice kit.

Sausage: Basque
Basic Sausage Recipe: Pork
Spice Kit:
1 teaspoon freshly floor black pepper 2 tablespoons piment d'Espelette
1 teaspoon toasted and floor aniseeds 1 dried bay leaf, floor
1 tablespoon minced garlic
Grind: Medium
Garnish:
¼ cup (60 ml) dry purple wine

Casing: Lamb
Sausage: Black Truffle Basic
Sausage Recipe: Pork Spice
Kit:
½ teaspoon freshly floor pepper
three allspice berries, floor
1 teaspoon minced garlic
Grind: Fine

Garnish:
ounce (30 g) sparkling black truffle, grated
tablespoons Cognac
Casing: Lamb or Pork

Sausage: Bordelaise
Basic Sausage Recipe: Pork
Spice Kit:
1½ teaspoons freshly floor pepper 2
tablespoons minced garlic
Grind: Fine

Garnish:
1½ cups (360 ml) dry purple wine decreased to ½ cup (a hundred and twenty ml)
¼ cup (15 g) chopped sparkling flat-leaf parsley
Casing: Lamb

Sausage: Breakfast
Basic Sausage Recipe: Pork
Spice Kit:
1½ teaspoons freshly floor black pepper
1 teaspoon floor cayenne
⅛ teaspoon freshly grated
nutmeg 1 allspice berry, floor
1 tablespoon minced garlic
Grind: Medium

Garnish:
½ cup (30 g) finely chopped sparkling sage
Casing: Lamb

Sausage: Calabrese
Basic Sausage Recipe: Pork

Spice Kit:

¼ cup (25 g) toasted and floor fennel seeds

tablespoons toasted and floor cumin seeds 2

teaspoons freshly floor black pepper

1 teaspoon freshly floor white pepper 2

tablespoons floor chile flakes

1 ½ teaspoons floor dried oregano

2 tablespoons minced garlic Grind: Fine Garnish:

¼ cup (60 ml) dry white wine

Casing: Pork

Sausage: Farmer's Sausage

Basic Sausage Recipe: Pork Spice Kit: 1 ½

teaspoons freshly floor black pepper 1

teaspoon toasted and floor aniseeds

1 teaspoon floor cayenne

Grind: Medium

Garnish:

1 ½ cups (360 ml) dry purple wine decreased to ½ cup (a

hundred and twenty ml) 1 tablespoons grated Pecorino

Romano cheese

Casing: Pork

Sausage: Fennel

Basic Sausage Recipe: Pork

Spice Kit:

2 tablespoons toasted and floor fennel seeds

1 ½ teaspoons freshly floor pepper

2 teaspoons floor dried oregano

four teaspoons minced garlic

Grind: Medium

Garnish:

½ cup (30 g) chopped sparkling flat-leaf

parsley 2 tablespoons entire fennel seeds,

toasted tablespoon chile flakes

¼ cup (60 ml) dry white wine

Casing: Lamb

Sausage: Lemon and Herb

Basic Sausage Recipe: Pork

Spice Kit:
1 ½ teaspoons toasted and floor coriander 2
dried bay leaves, floor
Grind: Fine
Garnish:
Grated zest of two lemons
¼ cup (60 ml) dry white wine
½ cup (30 g) chopped clean herbs, which include flat-leaf parsley,
chives, thyme, oregano, or sage
Casing: Lamb
Sausage: Merguez
Basic Sausage Recipe: Lamb
Spice Kit:
1 ½ teaspoons toasted and floor cumin seeds 1 ½
teaspoons toasted and floor coriander seeds 1
teaspoon freshly floor black pepper
1 teaspoon toasted and floor fennel seeds
big name anise, toasted and floor
allspice berries, toasted and floor
1 tablespoon plus ½ teaspoon paprika
⅛ teaspoon floor cinnamon
1   tablespoons   floor
cayenne Grind: Fine
Garnish:
Grated zest of ½ lemon blended with 1 tablespoon olive oil
Casing: Lamb
Sausage: Rabbit Boudin
Basic Sausage Recipe: Rabbit or Pork
Spice Kit:
1 teaspoon freshly floor white pepper
1 ½ teaspoons floor yellow mustard seeds 1
tablespoon floor dried thyme
1 ½ teaspoons piment d'Espelette
Grind: Fine, two
times Garnish:
None Casing: Lamb
Sausage: Spicy Italian

Basic Sausage Recipe: Pork

Spice Kit:

three tablespoons toasted and floor fennel

seeds I teaspoon freshly floor black pepper

$\frac{1}{2}$ teaspoon freshly floor white pepper

four teaspoons floor chile flakes

I tablespoon plus $\frac{1}{2}$ teaspoon paprika

I tablespoon minced garlicGrind: Medium Garnish:

2 tablespoons dry white wine

Casing: Pork

Sausage: Sweet Italian Basic

Sausage Recipe: Pork Spice

Kit:

I tablespoons toasted and floor fennel seeds I $\frac{1}{2}$

teaspoons toasted and floor aniseeds

three allspice berries, floor

I teaspoon freshly floor pepper I

tablespoon floor dried oregano I

tablespoon minced garlic

Grind: Medium

Garnish:

$\frac{1}{2}$ cup (30 g) chopped clean flat-leaf parsley

$\frac{1}{4}$ cup (60 ml) dry white wine

Casing: Pork

Sausage: Toulouse

Basic Sausage Recipe: Pork

Spice Kit:

I $\frac{1}{2}$ teaspoons freshly floor pepper

three complete cloves, floor

$\frac{1}{8}$ teaspoon freshly grated

nutmeg five allspice berries,

floor

2 tablespoons minced garlic

Grind: Medium

Garnish: None

Casing: Pork

Sausage: Wild Mushroom Basic

Sausage Recipe: Pork Spice Kit:
1 ½ teaspoons freshly floor pepper 2
allspice berries, floor
1 dried bay leaf, floor
1 teaspoon sweet (dulce) pimentón
Grind: Fine
Garnish:
cup (163 g) sautéed wild mushrooms
tablespoons chopped clean thyme
2 tablespoons chopped clean flat-leaf parsley
¼ cup (60 ml) dry crimson wine
Casing: Lamb

Stuffed Sausage

Stuffing sausage has historically been the herbal final results of sensible butchery. "Waste not, need not" became the chant of our ancestors, and so all the random bits and portions had been seasoned, floor, and crammed into the animal's intestines. If you have become severe approximately your sausage, you'll need to attempt your hand on the timehonored craft of casing sausage. Stuffing your sausage takes it to

the subsequent level. Loops, coils, hyperlinks of various lengths, and treasured packets wrapped in webby caul fats are the hallmark of state-of-the-art butchers and charcutiers. With a bit practice, you may crank out an array of meaty beauties and maintain the age-antique tradition.

Sausage Casings

Natural casings are the processed lamb, pork, and pork intestines used for casing sausage and salami. Somewhat permeable, they permit the fragrance of smoke or the taste of a poaching liquor to penetrate the beef even as their contents stay juicy and secure. Natural casings are available a whole lot of exceptional diameters (expressed in metric units; 1 inch equals 25 mm) to fit your desires and may be bought from a area of expertise butcher or sausage deliver company (see Sources).

The lamb, pork, and pork casings are normally bought packed in salt or brine. Before they may be used, they ought to be rinsed very well in numerous modifications of bloodless water. Once rinsed, they may be saved immersed in water withinside the fridge for as much as five days. For longer storage, drain them, % them in great sea salt, and refrigerate them for up to six months.

The casings that comply with are the maximum typically used withinside the charcuterie, and those used in the course of the recipes of this book.

Lamb Casings: Lamb casings are the maximum sensitive herbal intestinal casings, and that they generally tend to require a touch extra exercise and attention. They are commonly offered in distinct diameters: 22 to 24 mm, used for breakfast hyperlinks or merguez, and 24 to 26 mm, additionally called a frankfurter casing, typically used for decent dogs. Lamb casings are offered through the hank (a hundred feet/30 m), however you may frequently buy smaller portions from an excellent butcher. You will want approximately four feet (1.2 m) of lamb casing for each pound (450 g) of meat.

Hog Casings: Hog or red meat casings are the maximum common, versatile, and easy-to-use herbal casing. They are historically used for lots distinct kinds of sausages, which includes maximum Italian sausages, kielbasa, and boudin noir. Hog casings are available in loads of sizes. The 32 to 35 mm length is a superb all-cause casing for maximum sausages. They are offered through the hank (a hundred feet/30 m), however you may commonly purchase smaller

portions from an excellent butcher. You will want approximately 2 feet (60 cm) of hog casing for each pound (450 g) of meat.

Beef Middles and Sewn Beef Middles: Beef middles are a herbal a part of the pork gut historically used for salami and cotechino. They are normally offered through the piece and may be so long as 10 feet (three m). Plan on the usage of approximately 1 foot (30 cm) of pork center for each pound (450 g) of sausage.

Sewn pork middles, additionally called stitched pork middles, are pork middles which have been bolstered and closed at one end, making them very strong and ideal for medium-length cured salami. Like the ordinary middles, they're offered through the piece, however they're a good deal extra expensive.

Both kinds of middles come packed in salt and want to be very well rinsed in numerous modifications of water then soaked overnight. Be positive to show the middles internal out earlier than the usage of to show their clean interior. Once rinsed, they may be saved in water withinside the fridge for as much as five days. For longer storage, middles have to be drained, salted, and frozen.

Beef caps: Beef caps, or bungs, are every other a part of the herbal pork gut. Much large in diameter than middles, they're the conventional preference for mortadella and different massive salami. They are commonly offered through the piece, and aleven though they variety in length, maximum caps can maintain approximately 7 pounds (three.2 kg) of meat.

Beef caps come packed in salt and want to be very well rinsed in numerous modifications of water then soaked overnight. As with pork middles, you have to flip caps internal out previous to the usage of to show their clean interior. Once rinsed, they may be saved in water withinside the fridge for as much as five days. For longer storage, caps have to be drained, salted, and frozen.

Caul Fat: Caul fats is the lacy, weblike fats harvested from across the red meat liver historically used to line terrines or wrap crépinettes and different "uncased" sausages into neat packets. Extremely strong and versatile, it may be bought sparkling or frozen. Unlike gut casings, it isn't offered salted, however it nonetheless have to be properly rinsed to rid it of any last blood after which squeezed dry earlier than the usage of. You will want

approximately 1 pound (450 g) of caul fats to wrap three to four pounds (1.four to 1.eight kg) of meat.

Any unused caul fats may be saved immersed in water with a touch white vinegar for as much as five days. For longer storage, squeeze out as a good deal water as feasible and freeze.

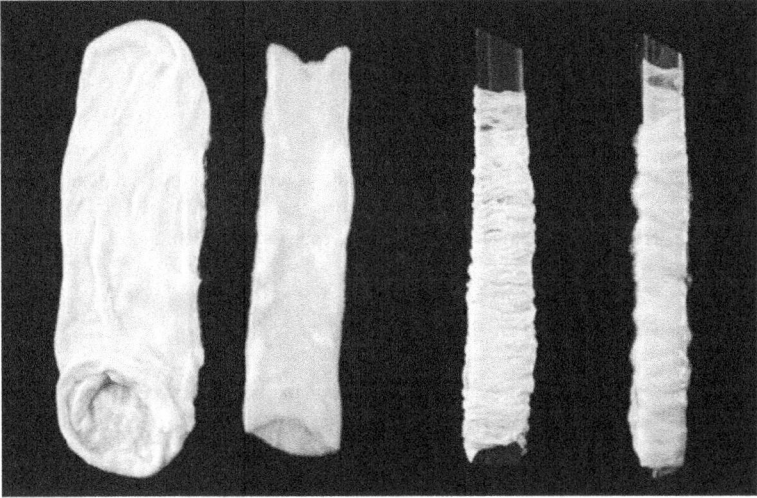

From left: pork cap/bung, pork center, hog casing, lamb casing

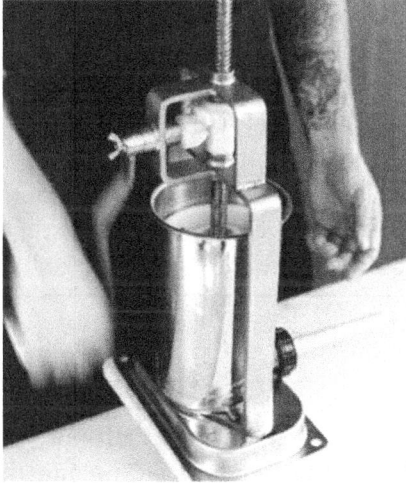

Stuffing and Linking Sausage

Stuffing and linking take exercise. Don't be discouraged in case your first few batches of sausage appearance a touch irregular. They will nonetheless flavor great. With exercise, your actions will improve, and earlier than you recognize it, you'll be cranking like a pro.

Assembling the Stuffer

1. Set the bottom on a piece surface. A damp towel or C-clamp will assist to preserve the stuffer in location as you work.

2. Screw the lid onto the piston.

3. Attach the cope with and rotate it till the lid ascends to its topmost position.

4. Transfer the sausage meat into the canister the usage of your hands, packing it down firmly every time.

5. Set the canister into the bottom.

6. Place a baking pan or tray beneath the nozzle to maintain the completed sausage as you stuff. You at the moment are prepared to stuff.

BLOW OUTS

Blowouts happen. Even people who have been making sausage for years experience the explodingsausage phenomenon. If you don't bust the occasional casing, you are probably not filling the casing tightly enough. When a casing does burst, simply squeeze the farce from the casing and set it aside. Cut away and discard the damaged portion of the casing, slip the new end of the casing over the nozzle, and continue to case. Reload the reserved farce into the stuffer at the next opportunity; make sure the casing isn't knotted at the

end of the nozzle to avoid trapping air as you reload the canister.

Stuffing

There will constantly be a small quantity of sausage left withinside the backside of the canister and withinside the nozzle that won't make it into the casing. This greater farce may be rolled into little meatballs, flattened into patties and grilled like burgers, delivered to soups, or used as a stuffing for veggies or roasts.

1. Remove a duration of soaked casing from the water. Open one give up and pour approximately 1 tablespoon water into the casing to lubricate. Thread the whole duration of casing onto the nozzle.

2. Turn the crank in order that the lid presses lightly onto the pinnacle of the beef, forcing just

    ½ inch (12 mm) of the beef out via the nozzle. This enables to dispose of air pockets.

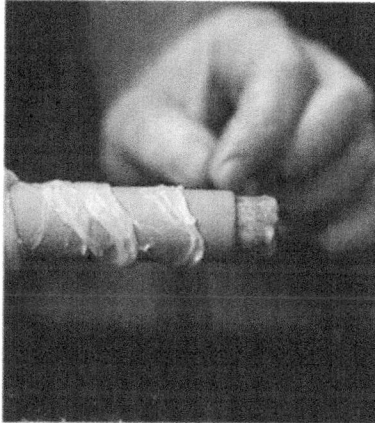

3. Pull the give up of the casing over the brink of the nozzle, then knot the give up of the casing. If you're the usage of sewn red meat middles or red meat caps, bypass the knot, as they may be already closed on the give up.

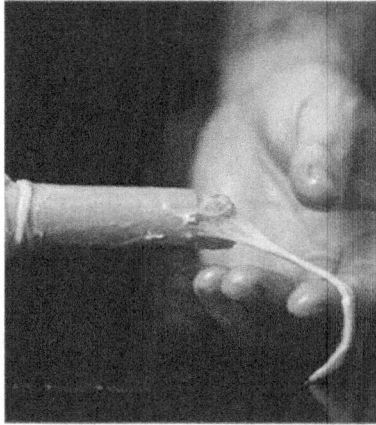

4. Place your thumb and forefinger across the give up of the nozzle to adjust the motion ofthe casing.

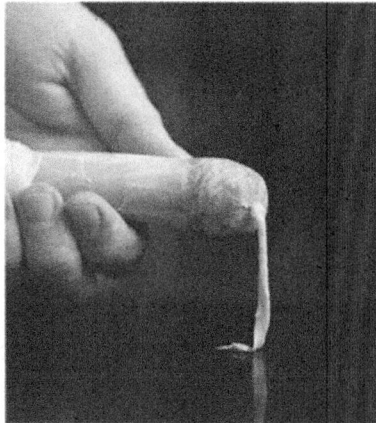

5. Crank the handle slowly to press the sausage meat into the casing. Release more casing off the nozzle as the sausage flows through the tube.

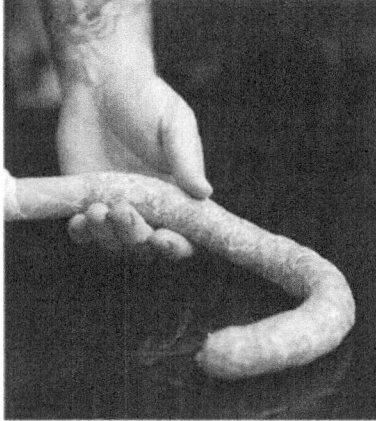

6. If an air bubble forms, prick the sausage casing with the tines of a sausage knife to releaseit. If you start to run out of casing, pause. Leave your self as a minimum three inches (7.five cm) of unstuffed casing and do away with the duration from the nozzle. Continue with a brand new duration of casing.

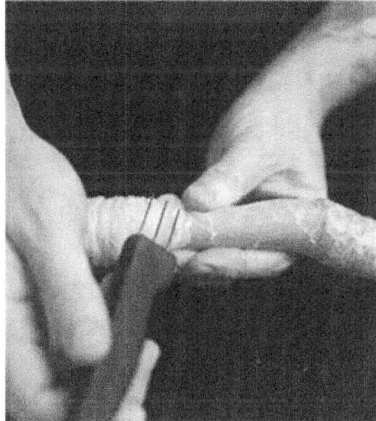

Linking

Once all your sausage is cased, you may start the system of linking. You could make hyperlinks in each hog and lamb casings in lots of sizes.

1. Decide the duration of your sausages. Cut a duration of wire to the preferred duration of your character sausage hyperlinks to apply as a manual.

2. Use the manual to pinch off your first duration of sausage. Align the string with the knotted give up of crammed casing and pinch down together along with your thumb and forefinger to split the primary hyperlink from the crammed casing.

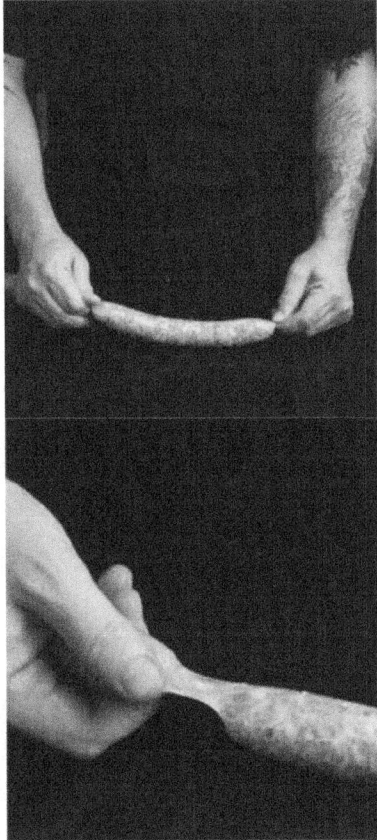

3. Twist to steady the hyperlink. Rotate the hyperlink farfar from you approximately seven times.

4. Start a 2d hyperlink. Move the string to align with the give up of the primary hyperlink to create the second one hyperlink.

5. Using the string as a manual, pinch off the second one hyperlink. Pinch down on the give up of the second one hyperlink, then rotate towards you approximately seven times.

6. Continue linking. Repeat this system alternating the course of rotation with every hyperlink.

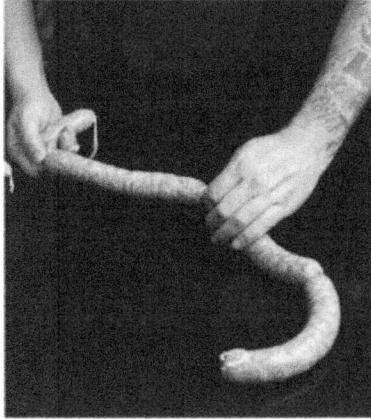

7. Separate the hyperlinks. When all the sausage has been cased, snip among every hyperlink with scissors leaving a little "tail" on both give up of every sausage to save you the farce from spilling out for the duration of cooking. If you may be striking your sausage overnight, maintain the hyperlinks connected in lengths of 4 to eight, and grasp every duration in a refrigerated location.

Coiling

Instead of linking the sausage, you may shape astonishing coils that make smooth paintings of grilling. Thinner coils are made with lamb casing, and truly thicker coils are made with hog casing. To set the coils, you'll want steel or bamboo skewers which can be as a minimum 10 inches (25 cm) long.

1. Soak the skewers. If you're the usage of bamboo skewers, soak them in cool water for as a minimum 30 minutes.

2. Link the sausage. Follow the instructions for making hyperlinks, however pinch off and rotate lengths of 18 to 24 inches (forty five to 60 cm), then snip

apart with scissors as directed.

3. Start coiling. With one hand, press one tail give up of casing onto your paintings floor to create a middle factor and maintain it firmly. Then, with the alternative hand, tightly wind the sausage across the middle factor.

4. Secure the coil. Pierce the outer give up of the casing (approximately ½ inch/12 mm from the tail of the hyperlink) with the pointed give up of the skewer and insert the skewer without delay via the middle of the coil, parallel to the paintings floor.

5. Skewer again. Rotate the coil ninety ranges and run a 2d skewer without delay via the middle of the coil.

Looping

Sausage that you may be striking for smoking or air-drying is regularly cased in loops, which paintings first-rate if hog casings had been used.

1. Prepare to case your sausage. Pull approximately 1 inch (2.five cm) of the give up of the casing over the outlet of the nozzle and knot.

2. Cut a 5-inch (12 cm) length of butcher's twine. Tie it directly below the knot.

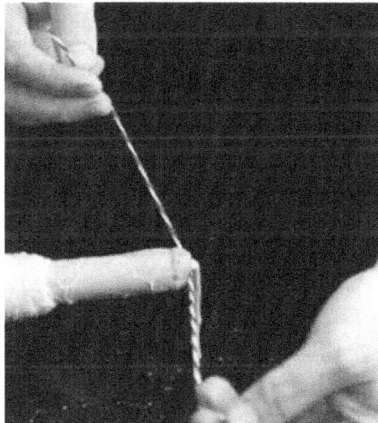

3. Stuff the sausage. Crank the cope with slowly to press the sausage meat into the casing to shape an 18-inch (forty six cm) duration. You will need to stuff hyperlinks to be looped greater completely and firmly than you stuff normal hyperlinks.

4. Loop the sausage. With one give up nonetheless connected to the nozzle, shape the hyperlink right into a loop.

5. Tie. Tie the 2 ends collectively with the free ends of the wire, then support with a 2d knot.

6. Loop the wire. Create a loop of wire 1 inch (2.five cm) in diameter through knotting the 2 free ends of wire. You will use this wire loop to grasp your looped sausage.

7. Start a 2d loop. Pull 2 inches (five cm) of empty casing off of the nozzle and tie a knot with a brand new five-inch (12 cm) duration of wire to start the subsequent loop. Then, the usage of scissors, sever the primary loop.

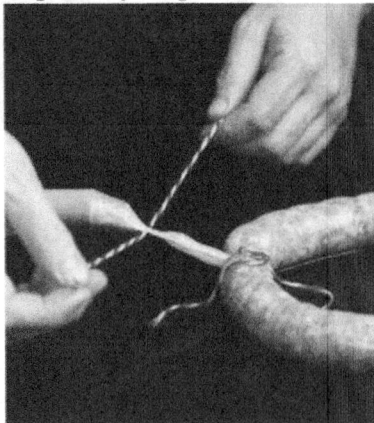

Wrapping

Wrapping sausage in caul fats is a tremendous opportunity to the usage of casings, specially in case you are creating a small quantity for clean intake or do now no longer have get entry to to a sausage stuffer.

1. Divide the sausage. Using a scale, divide the unfastened sausage into equalsize portions. In general, four to five ounces (a hundred and fifteen to a hundred and forty ounces) is a great component size.

2. Shape the sausage meat via way of means of hand into patties ¾ inch (2 cm) thick, smoothing the rims and casting off any cracks.

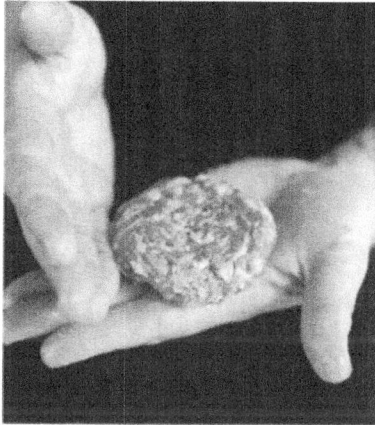

3. Prep the caul fats. Remove a bit of caul fats from the water and squeeze nicely to put off any extra water. Spread the caul fats out on a piece surface.

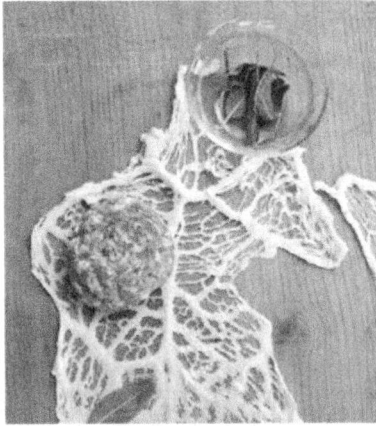

4. Lay the sausage patties at the caul fats, leaving a 2-inch (five cm) border of caul fats round every patty.

5. Wrap. Pull the threshold of the caul fats over the patties. Cut the caul fats across the patties. Trim any overlapping caul fats, then pinch to shut the seam.

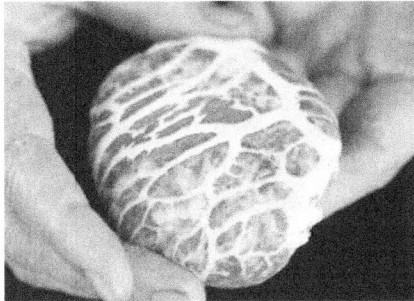

Cooked Sausage

Many conventional sausages are completed with a further cooking step, together with poaching or smoking. From wealthy blood sausage to smoky kolbász, sensitive bockwurst to snappy warm hyperlinks, the manner of cooking is used to impart flavor, offer texture, and assist to keep the sausage.

Poaching

Poaching is used to set or corporation the feel of a sausage with a moist or tender farce, a step that lets in it to be cooked effects at every other point. Some sausages are poached without delay following casing; others are higher if they're poached after being hung overnight.

Heat a massive pot of water earlier than you start grinding your meat. A 12quart (11.four L) stockpot will easily accommodate a five-pound (2.three kg) batch of sausage. Do now no longer allow the water come to a boil; instead, hold it simply beneath a simmer. Season the water with salt. For each four quarts (three.eight L) water, upload three tablespoons quality sea salt.

Grind, case, and hyperlink your sausage, however go away the hyperlinks connected instead of clipping them apart. Insert a thermometer to test the temperature of the poaching water. The most advantageous temperature is ready 160°F (70°C).

Transfer the hyperlinks to the pot and permit them to poach gently. Meanwhile, put together a massive ice-water tubtub. To make sure the hyperlinks prepare dinner dinner evenly, cautiously stir them each now and again. The overall cooking time is generally 15 to twenty minutes. The sausages are geared up while a thermometer inserted into the middle of a sausage registers a hundred and forty°F (60°C). Using a slotted spoon, put off the hyperlinks and vicinity them immediately into the ice-water tubtub to forestall the cooking and to assist to save you shrinkage.

When the links are thoroughly chilled, remove them from the ice bath and clip into individual links. Line a baking sheet or tray with a clean kitchen towel and place the links on the pan. Refrigerate uncovered overnight. The next day, transfer the sausages to an airtight container and return them to the refrigerator. Storage time varies from recipe to recipe, but its usually around 5 days.

THE SAUSAGE PARTY

Inviting over some sport buddies to enroll in you in making sausage can lighten the workload and make the manner even greater fun.

Ahead of time, determine what sorts of sausage you need to make. If that is the primary time for a few people, select simply one form of crammed sausage, or choose a clean sausage and crépinettes or patties. If you're vintage pros, select some distinct recipes, together with some thing that you'll poach or smoke. Decide who may be answerable for buying and collecting precise supplies, and mail order any unique supplies, together with casings or curing salt, if important. Make certain you've got got all the important gadget and that it's far in properly running order. Finally, set the time to get together.

One day earlier than you intend to meet, accumulate your supplies. Shop on your meat and different any components you'll need. Prepare your spice kits, then reduce your meat and marinate it.

Get together for the main event of grinding and casing.

BOCKWURST

Bockwurst is a traditional German sausage crafted from a combination of veal and beef and pro with clean herbs. Traditionally, it turned into eaten withinside the spring to accompany the wealthy, malty bock beer that were brewed via way of means of clergymen withinside the iciness months for consuming on the end of Lenten fasting. Although you may experience this wurst any time of year, some hyperlinks browned in butter or at the grill and served along inexperienced garlic mashed potatoes and a tall glass of darkish lager looks as if the best welcome to the spring season.

MAKES ABOUT 5½ POUNDS (2.FIVE KG) OR 18 TO 20 (6INCH/15 CM) LINKS

2½ pounds (1.2 kg) boneless veal shoulder, reduce into 1-inch (2.five cm) cubes

1¾ pounds (800 g) boneless beef picnic, reduce into 1-inch (2.five cm) cubes

12 ounces (340 g) beef again fats, reduce into 1inch (2.five cm) cubes

½ teaspoon white peppercorns

four complete cloves

¼ teaspoon mace blades

three allspice berries

2 tablespoons plus 1 teaspoon (1.four ounces/40g) quality sea salt

¼ teaspoon floor ginger **GARNISH**

3 eggs

1 cup (240 ml) heavy cream

½ cup (25 g) thinly sliced clean chives

¼ cup (15 g) chopped clean sage

Finely chopped zest of one lemon

10 quarts (9.five L) water pro with ½ cup (one hundred forty g) quality sea salt for poaching

10 feet (three m) organized hog casings

Place the veal, red meat, and fats in a massive nonreactive bowl or container. To make the spice package, in a spice grinder, integrate the pepper, cloves,

mace, and allspice and grind finely. Transfer to a small bowl and stir withinside the salt and ginger. Mix the spice package frivolously with the meat (see Basic Sausage Method), cover, and refrigerate overnight.

To collect the garnish, in a bowl, whisk collectively the eggs and cream till simply blended. Fold withinside the chives, sage, and lemon zest.

Refrigerate till geared up to use.

Refrigerate the elements of your grinder till geared up to use. Following the commands for grinding, suit the grinder with the smallest plate and grind the meats twice. Pour withinside the garnish and blend properly via way of means of hand for three minutes. The farce wishes to be blended mainly properly to hold the cream from isolating in the course of cooking. Cook a small pattern of the combination in a sauté pan and modify the seasonings if vital.

Fill a massive stockpot with the salted poaching water and warmth at the range pinnacle to 160°F (70°C).

Following the commands for Stuffing and Linking Sausage, stuff the farce withinside the hog casings and hyperlink into sausages approximately 6 inches (15 cm) long, leaving the sausages connected. Place the hyperlinks withinside the poaching water. It can be vital to modify the warmth, because the temperature will drop barely whilst you upload the hyperlinks to the pot. Poach the hyperlinks slowly for 15 to twenty minutes, till a thermometer inserted into the middle of a sausage registers one hundred forty°F (60°C). Meanwhile, put together a massive ice-water tubtub and line a baking sheet with a smooth kitchen towel.

When the hyperlinks are geared up, switch them to the ice-water tubtub for approximately 20 minutes, till properly chilled. Drain the hyperlinks, clip them apart, and set up them at the organized pan. Refrigerate exposed overnight. The subsequent day, wrap tightly in plastic wrap and refrigerate for as much as five days, or wrap cautiously and freeze for up to a few months.

Blood Sausage with Caramelized Apples and Cognac

BLOOD SAUSAGE WITH CARAMELIZED APPLES AND COGNAC

The sweetness of caramelized apples and slowly cooked onions mixed with the punch of Cognac and the earthiness of red meat and red meat blood make a first rate hyperlink in order to win over bloodsausage skeptics. The poached hyperlinks may be grilled;

sautéed with apples, potatoes, and onions; or sliced and

tucked among the layers of a root vegetable gratin.

MAKES ABOUT 7½ POUNDS (THREE.42KG) OR 22 TO 24 (6-INCH/15 CM) LINKS FORCEMEAT

2 cups (225 g) sliced yellow onions

I tablespoon unsalted butter

3 tablespoons plus 1½ teaspoons (2.1 ounces/fifty nine g) quality sea salt four pounds (1.eight kg) fatty red meat Boston butt, cutinto 1-inch (2.five cm) cubes

2 teaspoons peppercorns

three dried bay leaves

3 complete cloves

6 allspice berries

2 teaspoons piment d'Espelette

GARNISH

¼ cup (60 ml) lard or leaf lard

four cups (450 g) peeled and diced tart apples 1½ teaspoons quality sea salt

¼ cup (15 g) chopped clean thyme (stems reserved)

½ cup (a hundred and twenty ml) Cognac

four cups (960 ml) red meat blood, properly chilled

12 ounces (340 g) red meat returned fats, reduce into ¼inch (6 mm) cubes

PANADE

½ cup (30 g) clean bread crumbs

I cup (240 ml) heavy cream

COURT BOUILLON

10 quarts (9.five L) water

½ cup (one hundred forty g) quality sea salt

½ yellow onion, sliced

1½ teaspoons peppercorns

five dried bay leaves

Reserved thyme stems

15 feet (four.five m) organized hog casings

To make the forcemeat, integrate the onions and butter in a sauté pan set over low heat. Season with ½ teaspoon of the salt and sweat the onions slowly for approximately 20 minutes, till they're pretty soft and translucent. Remove from the warmth and allow cool.

Place the red meat in a massive nonreactive bowl or container. To make the spice package, in a spice grinder, integrate the peppercorns, bay, cloves, and allspice berries and grind finely. Transfer to a small bowl and stir withinside the piment d'Espelette and the last salt. Mix the spice package and cooled onions frivolously with the meat (see Basic Sausage Method), cover, and refrigerate overnight.

To make the garnish, in a huge sauté pan, soften the lard over medium-excessive warmth. When it starts to sizzle, upload the apples and prepare dinner dinner, stirring occasionally, for approximately 10 mins till they may be a wealthy golden brown. Add the salt and thyme and prepare dinner dinner for 1 minute longer. Remove from the warmth, pour withinside the Cognac, and stir with a wood spoon to loosen the fond from the lowest of the pan. Set apart to chill to room temperature. Reserve the blood and returned fats withinside the fridge till needed.

To make the panade, in a bowl, blend collectively the bread crumbs and cream.

To make the courtroom docket bouillon, in a huge stockpot, integrate the water, salt, onion, peppercorns, bay, and thyme stems. Place over low warmth and warmth to 160°F (70°C).

Refrigerate the elements of your grinder till geared up to use. Following the commands for grinding, match the grinder with the medium plate and grind the beef once. Pour withinside the red meat blood observed via way of means of the panade and blend nicely. Fold withinside the returned fats and the apples with their cooking juices. Mix the farce via way of means of hand, the usage of a quick, eggbeater-like rotating motion, for approximately 2 mins, till it holds collectively and tightens somewhat. This farce could be a piece looser than different sausage forcemeats. Cook a small pattern of the combination in a sauté pan and taste. It ought to be wealthy, nicely seasoned, and a tad spicy, with lots of taste from the apple and Cognac.

Following the commands for Stuffing and Linking Sausage, stuff the farce withinside the hog casings and hyperlink into sausages approximately 6 inches (15 cm) long, leaving the sausages connected. Place the hyperlinks withinside the courtroom docket

bouillon. It can be important to modify the warmth, because the temperature will drop barely while you upload the hyperlinks to the pot. Poach the hyperlinks slowly for approximately 25 to 30 mins, till a thermometer inserted into the middle of a sausage registers 150°F (66°C). Meanwhile, put together a huge ice-water tubtub and line a baking sheet with a smooth kitchen towel. When the hyperlinks are geared up, switch them to ice-water tubtub for approximately 20 mins, till nicely chilled. Drain the hyperlinks, clip them apart, and set up them at the organized pan. Refrigerate exposed overnight. The subsequent day, switch to an hermetic box and refrigerate for as much as five days, or wrap cautiously and freeze for up to two months.

Cotechino

COTECHINO

When wintry weather is withinside the air and the vacations are upon us, *cotechino makes its seasonal look at the chalkboard on the Fatted Calf.* A forte of northern Italy, *cotechino has a unique,* springy texture because of the uncommon addition of cooked red meat pores and skin. Although this huge, gently fermented sausage is scrumptious year-round, it's far historically brought to wintry weather favorites including Bollito Misto or simmered with lentils (as pictured) and eaten for precise good fortune on New Year's Day. (If you're serving the sausages with lentils, upload the lentils and any veggies or herbs to the pot approximately halfway thru cooking.) For a actually festive excursion version at the conventional cotechino, grate 1 ounce (30 g) clean black truffle and upload it to the farce after grinding.

MAKES ABOUT FIVE POUNDS (2.THREE KG) OR FIVE I-POUND (450 G) SAUSAGES

1¼ pounds (570 g) red meat pores and skin, reduce into strips I inch (2.five cm) wide

2 teaspoons coriander seeds

four allspice berries

1½ teaspoons black peppercorns

I teaspoon white peppercorns

four pounds (1.eight kg) red meat Boston butt, reduce into I-inch (2.five cm) cubes

2 tablespoons plus I teaspoon (1.four ounces/40g) nice sea salt I teaspoon curing salt no. I

⅛ teaspoon floor cinnamon 1 teaspoon floor ginger

¼ cup (60 ml) dry white wine

five feet (1.five m) organized pork middles, became interior out

Bring a huge stockpot full of water to a rolling boil. Add the red meat pores and skin and prepare dinner dinner for 10 mins. Drain and pat dry with paper towels, then switch to a bowl, cover, and refrigerate for 1 hour.

Preheat the oven to 325°F (165°C). Spread the coriander seeds on a baking sheet and toast for three to five mins, till fragrant. Let cool completely, then switch to a spice grinder, upload the allspice and black and white peppercorns, and grind finely.

Place the red meat in a huge nonreactive bowl or box. To make the spice package, in a small bowl, integrate the freshly floor spices, sea salt, curing salt, cinnamon, and ginger and blend nicely. Mix the spice package and the chilled red meat pores and skin frivolously with the beef (see Basic Sausage Method), cover, and refrigerate overnight.

Refrigerate the components of your grinder till geared up to use. Following the commands for grinding, healthy the grinder with the medium plate and grind the beef once. Pour withinside the wine and blend the farce via way of means of hand for two minutes, till it companies and holds together. Following the commands for salami, stuff the farce into the red meat middles. Hang the sausages in a cool, dry room for three days, then wrap loosely in a kitchen towel and refrigerate. They will hold for up to at least one week.

To prepare dinner dinner the sausages, fill a huge stockpot with gently salted water and warmth to approximately 165°F (74°C). Add the sausages and simmer for two hours.

BELGIAN BEER SAUSAGE

A rich, delicately hopped Belgian-fashion amber or blonde ale is prime to the fulfillment of this sausage. Belgian-fashion beers generally tend to have a creamy mousse, nearly tropical aroma, and diffused flavors of ginger, coriander, and caramel that marry delectably with red meat. Grill the completed hyperlinks and pinnacle with caramelized onions or brown in butter, then simmer with Traditional Sauerkraut and a dash of beer.

MAKES ABOUT FIVE POUNDS (2.THREE KG),OR 18 TO 20 LINKS (7-INCH/18 CM) LINKS

1 ½ teaspoons black peppercorns

2 teaspoons yellow mustard seeds

2 teaspoons coriander seeds

three allspice berries

2 tablespoons plus 1 teaspoon (1.four ounces/40g) pleasant sea

salt

1 teaspoon curing salt no. 1

2 teaspoons mild brown sugar

½ teaspoon floor mace

½ teaspoon floor cayenne

¼ teaspoon floor ginger 1

tablespoon minced garlic

¼ teaspoon finely chopped orange zest

3¾ pounds (1.7 kg) boneless red meat picnic, reduce into 1-inch (2.five cm) cubes

1¼ pounds (570 g) red meat lower back fats, reduce into 1inch (2.five cm) cubes 1¼ cups (three hundred ml) Belgian-fashion beer, nicely chilled

10 quarts (9.five L) water pro with ½ cup (one hundred forty g) pleasant sea salt for poaching

10 feet (three m) organized hog casings

Preheat the oven to 325°F (165°C). Spread the peppercorns, mustard and coriander seeds, and allspice on a baking sheet and toast for three to five minutes, till fragrant. Let cool completely, then switch to a spice grinder and grind finely.

To make the spice package, in a small bowl, integrate the freshly floor spices, sea salt, curing salt, brown sugar, mace, cayenne, ginger, garlic, and orange zest and blend nicely. Place the red meat and fats in a huge nonreactive bowl. Mix the spice package frivolously with the beef (see Basic Sausage Method), cover, and refrigerate overnight.

Refrigerate the components of your grinder till geared up to use. Following the commands for grinding, healthy the grinder with the smallest plate and grind the beef twice. Line a huge tray with parchment paper. Divide the farce into approximately 1-pound (450 g) portions, flatten every component right into a patty approximately 1 inch (2.five cm) thick, and region the patties on a parchment-covered tray. You need to have five patties. Freeze for approximately 1 hour, till now no longer pretty frozen however crunchy on the edges.

Prepare to emulsify the sausage. Refrigerate the bowl and blade of a meals processor for at the least 30 minutes, or region them withinside the freezer for at the least 15 minutes. When they may be nicely chilled, affix the bowl to the bottom of the processor and fasten the blade. Remove 1 sausage patty

from the freezer, wreck it into kind of 1-inch (2.five cm) chunks, and positioned them withinside the meals processor. Process for three minutes, slowly pouring in

¼ cup (60 ml) of the beer because the system is running. Turn off the processor, scrape the emulsified farce right into a huge bowl, and region the bowl withinside the fridge. Repeat the manner with the ultimate sausage patties. It is crucial that the beef and the system stay as bloodless as viable even as you work, so as to emulsify the sausage properly. If the meals processor starts to sense hot, pause and relax the whole lot once more for at the least 20 minutes. When all the farce has been processed, stir to combine nicely. Cook a small pattern of the aggregate in a sauté pan and regulate the seasonings if necessary.

Following the commands for Stuffing and Linking Sausage, case the farce withinside the hog casings and hyperlink into sausages approximately 7 inches (18 cm) long, leaving the hyperlinks connected. Then reduce into bunches of four hyperlinks every, and cling every bunch from an S hook withinside the fridge overnight.

The following day, fill a massive stockpot with the salted poaching water, vicinity over low warmness and warmth to 160°F (70°C). Place the four-hyperlink bunches withinside the poaching water. It can be important to modify the warmness, because the temperature will drop barely while you upload the hyperlinks to the pot. Poach the hyperlinks slowly for 15 to twenty minutes, till a thermometer inserted into the middle of a sausage registers 140°F (60°C).

Meanwhile, put together a massive ice-water tubtub and line a baking sheet with a easy kitchen towel.

When the hyperlinks are ready, switch them to the ice-water tubtub for approximately 20 minutes, till properly chilled. Drain the hyperlinks, clip them apart, and set up them at the organized pan. Refrigerate exposed in a single day. The subsequent day, wrap tightly in plastic wrap and refrigerate for up to ten days.

Hot Smoking

Hot smoking slowly chefs sausage, imbuing it with the impossible to resist taste of wooden smoke. Smoking additionally has the introduced bonus of retaining sausage with the aid of using protecting the floor with bacteriostatic and

mycostatic compounds that paintings to inhibit the increase of undesirable micro organism and molds.

Case your farce in loops or hyperlink in lengths of 4 sausages and grasp in a single day withinside the fridge to assist to shape a pellicle. The pellicle is the skinny pores and skin or glaze shaped with the aid of using drying that seals the floor of the sausage, supporting the smoke adhere and preserving the indoors of the sausage wet for the duration of smoking.

Prepare your smokehouse following the suggestions for Hot and Cold Smoking. When the smoker reaches a temperature of 170°F to 180°F (77°C to 82°C), grasp the sausages withinside the smoke-stuffed cabinet. Space them calmly approximately 2 inches (five cm) apart, and keep away from crowding to permit for even smoking. Most sausage will take approximately an hour to smoke fully. Sausages are cooked whilst a thermometer inserted into the middle of a sausage registers approximately 140°F (60°C).

If you intend on ingesting the sausages warm from the smoker, they're now ready. If you intend on storing them to consume later or to consume chilled, put together a massive ice-water tubtub and line a baking sheet with a easy kitchen towel. Remove the sausages from the smoker and vicinity them withinside the ice-water tubtub to forestall the cooking and to assist to save you shrinkage.

When they're very well chilled, eliminate them from the ice tubtub. If your sausage is in hyperlinks, clip them apart. Place the hyperlinks or loops at the organized pan and refrigerate exposed in a single day. The subsequent day, wrap tightly in plastic wrap and refrigerate for up to ten days.

KOLBÁSZ

Kolbász

There are many sorts of kolbász, the Hungarian phrase for "sausage." This smoked model with paprika is historically introduced to lesco, a Hungarian vegetable stew with tomatoes and peppers, however it's also amazing immediately from the smoker, with rye bread, pickled pink cabbage, and warm mustard.

MAKES ABOUT 5½ POUNDS (2.THREE KG) OR FIVE OR 6 LOOPS
2 teaspoons black peppercorns

I cardamom pod
I tablespoon dried oregano
2 tablespoons plus I teaspoon (I.four ounces/forty g) satisfactory sea salt
¼ cup (27 g) warm Hungarian paprika I teaspoon sugar
I teaspoon curing salt no. I
¼ teaspoon floor mace
2 tablespoons minced garlic
four pounds (I.eight kg) boneless beef picnic, reduce into I-inch (2.five cm) cubes
I pound (450 g) beef again fat, reduce into I inch (2.five cm) cubes I cup (240 ml) ice water
10 feet (three m) organized hog casings

Preheat the oven to 325°F (165°C). Spread the peppercorns on a baking sheet and toast for three to five minutes, till fragrant. Let cool completely, then switch to a spice grinder, upload the cardamom pod and oregano, and grind finely.

To make the spice package, integrate the freshly floor seasonings, sea salt, paprika, sugar, curing salt, mace, and garlic and blend properly. Mix the spice package calmly with the meat (see Basic Sausage Method), cover, and refrigerate in a single day.

Refrigerate the elements of your grinder till equipped to use. Remove the beef from the fridge rapidly earlier than you're equipped to grind. Separate approximately one-fourth of the leanest portions of red meat and set aside. Line a baking sheet with parchment paper. Following the commands for grinding, match the grinder with the smallest plate and grind all the fats and the last red meat twice. When the second one grinding is complete, forestall the grinder, transfer to the biggest plate, and coarsely grind the tilt red meat once. Combine all the red meat and blend properly with the aid of using hand for two to a few minutes, till the farce starts offevolved to organization up and experience cohesive. Transfer the farce to the organized baking sheet and flatten right into a huge patty approximately 1 inch (2.five cm) thick. Freeze for approximately 1 hour, till now no longer pretty frozen however crunchy on the edges.

Place 1/2 of of the in part frozen meat into the bowl of a stand mixer equipped with the paddle attachment and blend on low pace for 1 minute whilst slowly incorporating 1/2 of of the ice water. Once the water has been absorbed, beat on excessive pace for 1 minute. Scrape the paddled farce right into a bowl and set aside. Repeat the technique with the last 1/2 of of the beef, incorporating the relaxation of the ice water. Mix all of the beef collectively with the aid of using hand. Cook a small pattern of the combination in a sauté pan and alter the seasonings if necessary.

Case the farce in hog casings and shape into loops (see Stuffing and Linking Sausage). Hang every loop from an S hook in a groovy area or withinside the fridge overnight.

The following day, put together your smokehouse following the suggestions for Hot and Cold Smoking. When the smoker reaches a temperature of 180°F (82°C), prepare dinner dinner the sausages slowly for approximately 1 to 1½ hours, till a thermometer inserted into the middle of a loop registers 140°F (60°C). If you need to consume the sausages warm from the smoker, they may be now equipped. If you need to consume them later, put together a huge ice-water tubtub and line a baking sheet with a smooth kitchen towel. Place the sausages withinside the ice-water tubtub for approximately 30 minutes.

When they may be very well chilled, take away them from the ice tubtub, location them at the organized baking sheet, and refrigerate exposed overnight. The subsequent day, wrap tightly in plastic wrap and refrigerate for up to ten days.

Hot Links

HOT LINKS

Spicy red meat warm links, smoked slowly over a hardwood fire, are a Texas barbeque specialty. For a real Hill Country experience, smoke a brisket and some red meat ribs along those zesty, plump links.

MAKES ABOUT FIVE POUNDS (2.THREE KG) OR 18 TO 20 LINKS
2 teaspoons coriander seeds
2 teaspoons black peppercorns
three allspice berries, floor
2 tablespoons floor chile flakes
2 pounds (900 g) boneless lean red meat, reduce into 1-inch (2.five cm) cubes
2 pounds (900 g) boneless red meat Boston butt, reduce into 1-inch (2.five cm) cubes
2 pound (450 g) red meat returned fats, reduce into 1inch (2.five cm) cubes three tablespoons (1.2 ounces/34 g) first-class sea salt
1 teaspoon curing salt no. 1
2 teaspoons floor cayenne
three tablespoons minced
garlic 1 cup (240 ml) ice
water
10 feet (three m) organized hog casings

Preheat the oven to 325°F (165°C). Spread the coriander seeds on a baking sheet and toast for three to five minutes, till fragrant. Let cool completely, then switch to a spice grinder, upload the peppercorns, allspice, and chile flakes, and grind finely.

Place the red meat in a nonreactive bowl or container. Place the red meat and red meat fats in a 2nd nonreactive bowl or container. To make the spice package, integrate the freshly floor spices, sea salt, curing salt, cayenne, and garlic. Mix a bit much less than 1/2 of of the spice package with the red meat, then blend the last spice package with the red meat and fats. Cover each bowls and refrigerate overnight.

Refrigerate the elements of your grinder till equipped to use. Line a baking sheet with parchment paper. Following the commands for grinding, match the grinder with the smallest plate and grind the red meat combination twice. When the second one grinding is complete, forestall the grinder, transfer to the biggest plate, and coarsely grind the red meat once. Combine red meat and red meat combination and blend properly with the aid of using hand for two to a few minutes, till the farce starts offevolved to organization up and experience cohesive. Transfer the farce to the organized baking sheet and flatten right into a huge patty approximately 1 inch (2.five cm) thick. Freeze for 1 hour, till now no longer pretty frozen however crunchy on the edges. Meanwhile, sit back the bowl and paddle of your stand mixer withinside the fridge.

Place 1/2 of of the in part frozen meat into the bowl of the stand mixer geared up with the paddle attachment and blend on low pace for two mins at the same time as slowly incorporating 1/2 of of the ice water. Once the water has been absorbed, beat on excessive pace for two mins. Scrape the paddled farce right into a bowl and set aside. Repeat the procedure with the closing meat, incorporating the relaxation of the ice water. Mix all of the beef collectively via way of means of hand. Cook a small pattern of the combination in a sauté pan and alter the seasonings if necessary.

Following the commands for Stuffing and Linking Sausage, stuff the farce withinside the hog casings and hyperlink into sausages approximately 7 inches (18 cm) long, leaving the hyperlinks connected. Then reduce into bunches of four hyperlinks every, and cling every bunch from an S hook in a groovy area or withinside the fridge overnight.

The following day, put together your smokehouse following the recommendations for Hot and Cold Smoking. When the smoker reaches a temperature of 180°F (82°C), prepare dinner dinner the sausages for approximately 1 to 1½ hours, till a thermometer inserted into the middle of a hyperlink registers 140°F (60°C). Hot hyperlinks loved proper out of the smoker are a revelation. But in case you can not devour all of them at once, put together a massive icewater tubtub and line a baking sheet with a smooth kitchen towel. Remove the sausages from the smoker and location them withinside the ice-water tubtub for approximately 20 mins, till properly chilled.

When they're very well chilled, dispose of them from the ice tubtub, location them at the organized baking sheet, and refrigerate uncovered

overnight. The subsequent day, wrap tightly in plastic wrap and refrigerate for up to two weeks.

Dried Sausage and Salami

There is the technological know-how of curing, a complicated collaboration of herbal processes—an problematic dance finished at a microbial level. Then there may be the ardour for salami, a mystery choice to create an underground lair strung with lengths of drying sausages, the air redolent of garlic and a musty perfume. Somewhere among the technological know-how and the ardour lies the recipe for amazing salami.

Salami takes its call from the historic Greek metropolis of Salamis, which perished round 450 BCE. But its fashion of fermented dried sausage lived on and unfold from this coastal port throughout the Mediterranean. Salami is idea to have fueled the Roman legions, who similarly unfold its reputation at some stage in the empire, in which local possibilities and availability of components gave beginning to infinite variations.

Good salami is the end result of high-satisfactory components, right methods, a useful environment, a touch patience, and a sprint of top fortune. It takes the strategies of sausage making and exposes them to the mysteries of the herbal global with the hopes that during everywhere from weeks to 6 months you'll own a aspect of beauty.

Note: Although many cultures put together their own extraordinary variations of air-dried sausages, the Italian time period salami has been typically used as a catchall withinside the English-talking global. But In Italy, *salame (salami is the Italian plural) has a miles extra particular which means than what we typically ascribe to it withinside the United States.* In Italy, a salame is a massive dried cured sausage, and plenty of words (together with salametto or salsiccia secca) describe smaller dried cured sausage in beef or lamb casing. At the Fatted Calf, we use the phrase salami while regarding the grander class of "dried cured sausages"—however we additionally use it withinside the extra particular, Italian experience of the phrase (that is, to explain large air-dried sausages). For smaller dried cured sausages, which Italians would possibly name salametti or salsiccia secca, we appoint the time period dried sausage.

Meat and Fat

The meat blend for salami is typically leaner than that for sparkling or warm cooked sausage, approximately 20 percentage fats to eighty percentage lean. Most salami is crafted from beef or a mixture of beef and beef. Pork picnic shoulder or leg cuts frequently comprise sufficient intramuscular fats to make extra lower back fats unnecessary. Salami also can be made the use of different meats, together with wild boar, venison, or maybe duck and goose. For premier results, use meat that has been trimmed of seen fats and complement with beef lower back fats to gain the right ratio of meat to fats.

Seasoning and Grinding

Because dried sausages are fermented and cured as opposed to cooked, seasoning them have to be performed with precision. They want to include approximately three percentage salt plus extra curing salt. Both elements offer seasoning in addition to inhibit the increase of undesirable and threatening microorganisms. Curing salt additionally offers those sausages their attractive crimson color. For higher accuracy, salt is measured via way of means of weight as opposed to extent while making all styles of salami.

Spices offer wonderful taste profiles however additionally act as antioxidants and stimulate the increase of (good) lactic bacteria. Often a mixture of entire and floor spices is used for making salami. Herbs are usually used of their dried shape and are frequently floor in conjunction with the spices.

Grind the beef for salami simply as you will for clean and cooked sausage, however blend for a piece longer—three to four minutes. The salami farce desires to be blended properly with the intention to distribute elements calmly and to cast off air wallet that could purpose spoilage.

BASIC REC IPE FO R
SALAMI

4 pounds (1.8 kg) lean boneless pork or a mixture ofpork and beef
+ 1 pound (450 g) pork back fat
+ 4 tablespoons (2.4 ounces/68 g) fine sea salt
+ 1 teaspoon curing salt no. 2
—

4 pounds (2.3 kg) basic salami

Casing, Linking, Looping, and Tying

In general, the manner you case your salami might be decided via way of means of the kind of casing you operate. And the scale of the casing you operate will in element decide how lengthy you'll age your salami.

Small dried sausages in lamb or hog casings may be fashioned into hyperlinks much like clean sausage, however you'll need to percent the casings a touch extra completely earlier than striking them to dry in lengths of 4 to eight

hyperlinks. Similarly, you may use hog casings to make loops. Most dried sausage cased in lamb or hog casings might be geared up to consume in 2 or three weeks.

All red meat casings are pretty robust and make exquisite salami that may be hung for lots months.

If you're casing in red meat middles, sewn red meat middles, or red meat caps, cast off your properly-rinsed, soaked, and inverted casing from the soaking water and thread it onto the nozzle. See pics 1 via three for Casing, Linking, Looping, and Tying.

If you're the usage of regular, open-ended red meat middles, pull 1 inch (2.five cm) of the casing over the hole of the nozzle. Tie a 6-inch (15 cm) duration of cord across the cease of the casing. Wind every cease of the cord over the pinnacle and tie a 2d knot on the bottom to steady the primary knot. Create a loop 1 inch (2.five cm) in diameter via way of means of knotting the 2 unfastened ends of the cord (see image four). You will use this loop to cling your completed salami.

Crank the cope with slowly to press the sausage blend into the casing to shape a 12-inch (30 cm) link (see image five). Tie a 6-inch (15 cm) duration of cord right into a knot across the casing simply earlier than the cease of the filled casing. This will go away a small quantity of the stuffing on the alternative facet of the knot (see image 6). This guarantees that the salami is tightly cased and gets rid of an air hole on the cease. The stuffing on the alternative facet may be pressed away and used to begin the following salami. Wind every cease of the cord over the pinnacle and tie a 2d knot on the bottom to steady it. Create a loop 1 inch (2.five cm) in diameter via way of means of knotting the 2 unfastened ends of cord. This 2d loop is used as a fail-secure have to the primary loop come undone.

Tie a 6-inch (15-cm) duration of cord across the casing approximately 1 inch (2.five cm) from the cease of the nozzle to start your subsequent salami (see image 7). Wind every cease of cord over the pinnacle and tie a 2d knot on the bottom to steady it. Then, the usage of scissors, sever the primary salami. Begin stuffing the following salami and repeat the method till all the sausage blend is used.

For sewn middles and caps, the method is similar, however You'll now no longer want to tie an cease knot to start due to the fact one cease is already closed. You

can count on to get approximately massive sausages from every piece of sewn center or cap.

CASING, LINKING, LOOPING, AND TYING

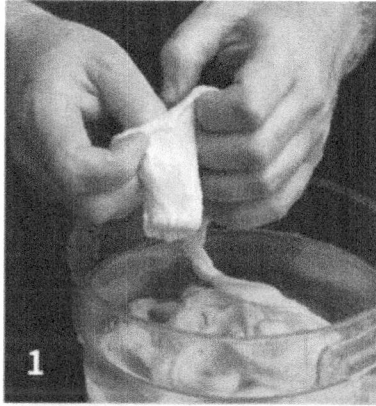

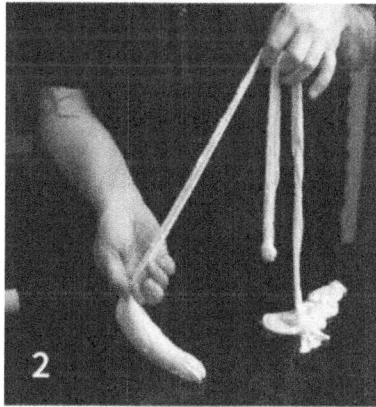

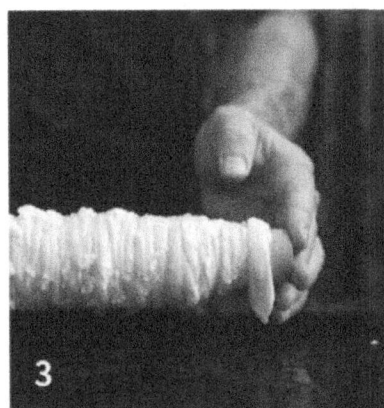

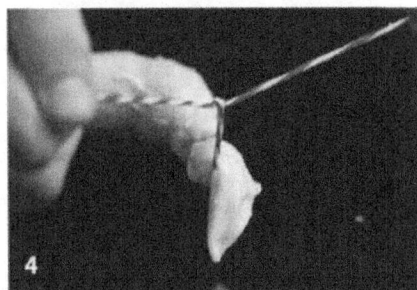

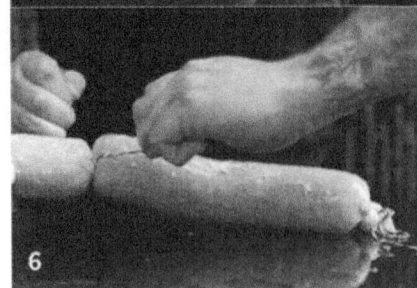

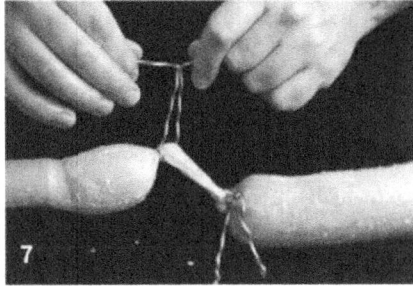

Hanging Salami for Initial Fermentation and for Drying

The uncooked sausage becomes "cured" or completed via way of means of present process a method of fermentation spawned via way of means of microorganisms that acidulate the sausage, that is, decrease its pH. Fermentation and curing aren't actual sciences. Temperature, humidity, and different environmental elements will have an effect on the outcome.

After your salami is cased, you'll want to cling it for a length at some stage in which the fermentation will begin. Warm and humid situations have a tendency to inspire the boom of the micro organism vital for fermentation. Ideally, a great place to cling salami has no daylight and a regular temperature of 65°F to 75°F (18°C to 24°C). Most dried sausages want to cling for three to five days, relying on the dimensions, ingredients, and the situations of the space (much less time in warmer, damper spaces; greater time in cooler, drier spaces). If you've got got a hydrometer, a nifty tool that measures the humidity, you're seeking to gain a degree of approximately 70 percent. If you stay in a place with very low tiers of humidity, keep in mind the usage of a popular domestic humidifier to enhance situations. If the situations are right, a whitish

bloom ought to seem at the outdoor of the casing in 2 or three days. This is the signal that fermentation has started.

If you do now no longer see a bloom, or if the salami begins offevolved to seem wrinkled withinside the first day or two, the surroundings is maximum probable too dry. Lightly mist the salami with water a few times at some stage in the preliminary fermentation length. For dried sausages in pork casings, a each day misting is often a right concept despite the fact that the environmental situations are right.

Check dried sausages in lamb or hog casings after three days. Their colour ought to be a brilliant rosy to reddish hue, relying at the spices used, and that they ought to have a pleasant odor. If they're touching one another, an extra of white mould may also form, and you may want to softly flip or separate them to enhance airflow. Hang them at room temperature or a piece cooler to complete drying. For salami in pork casings, take a look at after three or four days. Once a wholesome white bloom of mould seems at the salami, you'll need to transport it right into a cooler area, 50°C to 60°F (10°C to 16°C) for growing older from 2 to six months.

Allowing and cultivating mould to develop on our meals appears to counter what we've come to trust is right and safe, however the molds on salami paintings in particular at the outdoor, developing a barrier that enables to shield them in opposition to dangerous pathogens at some stage in the drying procedure.

PRESSING LARGE SALAMI

If you want large salami with a very firm texture, pressing after the initial fermentation can help. To press, simply lay the sausages on a tray lined with parchment paper. Lay another piece of parchment over the sausages, then place another tray on top of that. Weight the top tray with something dense and heavy that won't slide off (bricks wrapped in plastic wrap, full olive oil cans, or other rectangular weights are good options). Distribute the weight evenly and press for a week, then hang to cure.

Drying and Aging

The drying and growing older procedure is decided through the weather of the curing surroundings and the dimensions and fashion of the casing. After fermentation, the sausage needs to be dried. This modifications the casings from being water permeable to being moderately airtight, and the procedure is generally one in all a few trial and error. Unless you're a business salami producer with a relatively managed synthetic surroundings wherein you could effortlessly modify and display temperature and humidity, it's miles not going that you'll gain "perfect" situations. Focus much less on what you can't gain and greater on what you need to paintings with. Folks had been making salami lengthy earlier than the appearance of refrigeration, humidifiers, dehumidifiers, and the like, so it is able to be done. From drafty uninsulated attics to chill basements, from wine cellars to air-conditioned closets, humans have discovered methods to make it paintings.

The smaller the casing, the much less genuine the situations want to be.

Dried sausages in smaller hog or lamb casings dry greater quick and are much less challenge to environmental fluctuations. If you're making salami for the primary time or trying to make salami in a brand new location, make a small batch of dried sausage in lamb or hog casings to check out the situations of your space. How quick they dry, whether or not or now no longer the mould paperwork or how rapid it paperwork can clue you in at the relative feasibility.

Larger salami in pork casings require a touch greater paintings and care. They are preferably elderly round 50°F (10°C), however it's miles greater vital which you gain a regular temperature than an genuine one. You can age salami at temperatures as little as 40°F (four°C) and as excessive as 60°F (16°C), however huge fluctuations in temperature may be negative to the curing procedure.

Bacteria: The Good, the Bad, the Commercial

Making salami isn't not like making cheese. During the fermentation procedure, micro organism digest sugars (clearly taking place sugars from the beef plus any brought sugars) and bring lactic acid. Lactic acid lowers the pH and makes the beef an inhospitable surroundings for

undesirable micro organism. The lactic acid additionally imparts that tangy taste commonly related to salami.

Some human beings like to apply a industrial starter tradition or micro organism to assist to sell the fermentation technique and make certain a better charge of success. Commercial starters produce a fairly steady product however additionally have a propensity to regulate the taste of the salami, making it very tangy and protecting a number of the nuances of the flavors of the beef and spices.

You could make salami with out a industrial starter. Traditionally made salami rely upon wild lines of micro organism normally associated with Lactobacilli plantarum. These are the herbal plants gift all round us. Harnessing them may be a touch tricky, however we discover that the taste they supply salami is some distance advanced to what's viable with industrial starter cultures. Adding a small quantity of wine in your salami recipe is any other herbal manner to assist to begin the fermentation.

You might also additionally sometimes discover your self with a terrible stress of micro organism. White, gray, green, or even blue molds are wholesome and beneficial, however in case your salami is generating reddish or black mildew, don't take any chances. Discard it.

Finishing

Although a few signs can assist to decide the readiness of your salami, in fact your salami is accomplished whilst making a decision it's miles accomplished. Many styles of salami may be loved at diverse degrees of ripeness, from very younger and soft (the fashion recognised in Italian as morbido, loved in lots of elements of the country) to very corporation and dry. A dry salami will lose approximately 30 percentage of its authentic weight and need to yield barely however sense corporation whilst pressed together along with your fingertips. When you harvest your salami, wipe off any extra mildew and peel away the casing earlier than slicing. (Note which you do now no longer want to peel away the casing from dried sausage in hog or lamb casings.) When you slice right into a completed salami, it need to appearance brightly coloured and odor irresistible.

CACCIATORINI

Cacciatori are "hunters" in Italian, and cacciatorini are the little dried sausages that hunters can stash without difficulty of their wallet for fast sustenance all through their lengthy treks via the woods. *Cacciatorini are high-quality amusing to make and a great start line in case you are simply starting to discover ways to make salami.*

MAKES ABOUT THREE POUNDS (I.FOUR KG) OR 20 (FIVE-INCH/THIRTEEN CM) LINKS

I teaspoon aniseeds
I tablespoon black peppercorns
five kilos (2.three kg) boneless lean beef from shoulder or leg, reduce into I-inch (2.five cm) cubes
three tablespoons plus I½ teaspoons (2.I ounces/fifty nine g) first-rate sea salt I teaspoon curing salt no. 2
I½ tablespoons entire chile flakes
I tablespoon finely minced garlic
½ cup (one hundred twenty ml) purple wine
10 feet (three m) organized hog casings

Preheat the oven to 325°F (165°C). Spread the aniseeds on a baking sheet and toast for three to five minutes, till fragrant. Let cool completely, then switch to a spice grinder, upload the peppercorns, and grind finely. Place the beef in a massive nonreactive bowl or container. To make the spice package, in a small bowl, integrate the freshly floor spices, sea salt, curing salt, chile flakes, and garlic. Mix the spice package frivolously with the beef (see Basic Sausage Method), cover, and refrigerate overnight.

Refrigerate the elements of your grinder till prepared to apply. Following the commands for grinding, suit the grinder with the smallest plate and grind the beef once. Pour withinside the wine and blend nicely with the aid of using hand for three to four minutes, till the beef may be very corporation and all the wine is incorporated

Following the commands for Stuffing and Linking Sausage, stuff the farce tightly withinside the hog casings and hyperlink into sausages five inches (12 cm) lengthy, leaving the sausages connected. Separate every hyperlink from the subsequent with the aid of using tying off the hyperlinks with twine, then reduce into lengths of three hyperlinks. Hang in a appropriate area at or simply under room temperature (65°F to 70°F/18°C to 21°C is optimal) for 12 to fourteen days, till corporation sufficient to slice. The completed cacciatorini may be saved in a cool, dry spot for numerous months, to be loved on lengthy walks via the woods and different adventures.

SAUCISSE SEC AUX HERBES DE PROVENCE

These thin dried sausages pro with a great quantity of herbs are redolent of a summery meadow. They make a high-quality addition to a picnic basket.

MAKES ABOUT 24 (7½-INCH/19 CM) LINKS
five kilos boneless lean beef shoulder or leg, reduce into 1-inch (2.five-cm) cubes
1 tablespoon Herbes de Provence
1 teaspoon black peppercorns
1 teaspoon white peppercorns
2 tablespoons plus 2 teaspoons (1.6 ounces/forty six g)
sea salt 1 teaspoon curing salt no. 2
1 teaspoon fennel pollen or toasted and finely floor fennel seeds
1 tablespoon finely minced garlic
¼ cup (60 ml) dry white wine
20 feet (6 m) organized lamb casings, 22 to 24 mm in diameter

Place the beef in a massive nonreactive bowl or container. To make the spice package, in a spice grinder, integrate the herbes de Provence and the black and white peppercorns and grind finely. Transfer to a small bowl, upload the ocean salt, curing salt, fennel, and garlic, and blend nicely. Mix the spice package frivolously with the beef (see Basic Sausage Method), cover, and refrigerate overnight.

Refrigerate the components of your grinder till equipped to use. Following the commands for grinding, match the grinder with the smallest plate and grind the beef once. Pour withinside the wine and blend with the aid of using hand for approximately three to four minutes, till the beef may be very company and all the wine is absorbed. Following the commands for Stuffing and Linking Sausage, stuff the farce tightly withinside the lamb casings and hyperlink into sausages 7½ inches (19 cm) long, keeping apart every hyperlink with a chunk of twine. Cut into lengths of 6 hyperlinks. Hang in a appropriate region at or simply beneath room temperature (65°F to 70°F/18°C to 21°C is optimal), the usage of 1-inch (2.5cm) S hooks positioned among the second one and 1/3 hyperlinks and the fourth and 5th hyperlinks. Make positive not one of the hyperlinks is touching every other hyperlink. The sausages will dry in 1 to two weeks, relying at the ambient temperature. They are equipped whilst they're company sufficient to slice.

The completed sausages may be saved in a cool, dry spot for six weeks.

PEPPERONI

This spicy, sturdy salami will make you reconsider pepperoni. While it absolutely may be strewn atop pizza or nibbled with olives and cheese, you may additionally upload it to a salad of shaved fennel and arugula or sauté it with thinly sliced broccoli rabe.

MAKES ABOUT 7 POUNDS (THREE.2 KG) OR 10 TO 12 (10-INCH/25 CM) SAUSAGES

1½ teaspoons fennel seeds
½ teaspoon aniseeds
1 teaspoon peppercorns
eight allspice berries
10 pounds (four.five kg) boneless red meat chuck approximately eighty percentage lean meat and 20 percentage fat, reduce into 1-inch (2.five cm) cubes ounces (152 g) nice sea salt 2 teaspoons curing salt no. 2
2 tablespoons floor cayenne

3 tablespoons unsmoked Spanish paprika
three cloves garlic, pounded to a paste in a mortar with ½
teaspoon nice sea salt
¼ cup (60 ml) dry pink wine
10 feet (three m) organized red meat middles or sewn red
meat middles, rinsed and grew to become inner out

Preheat the oven to 325°F (165°C). Spread the fennel seeds and aniseeds on a baking sheet and toast for three to five minutes, till fragrant. Let cool completely, then switch to a spice grinder, upload the peppercorns and allspice, and grind finely.

Place the red meat in a massive nonreactive bowl or container. To make the spice package, in a small bowl, integrate the freshly floor spices, the ocean salt, curing salt, cayenne, paprika, and garlic and blend nicely. Mix the spice package frivolously with the beef (see Basic Sausage Method), cover, and refrigerate overnight.

Refrigerate the components of your grinder till equipped to use. Following the commands for grinding, match the grinder with the smallest plate and grind the beef twice. Pour withinside the wine and blend nicely with the aid of using hand for

4 to five minutes, till the beef may be very company and all the wine is nicely incorporated.

Following the commands for Casing, Linking, Looping, and Tying, stuff the farce withinside the red meat casings and hyperlink into sausages approximately 10 inches (25 cm) long, keeping apart every hyperlink as it's miles cased. Hang in a appropriate region with a temperature of 65°F to 70°F (18°F to 21°F) for three to four days, till the salami has grew to become a deep pink and indicates the beginnings of a white bloom at the casing. Then circulate to a cooler region (50°F/10°C might be optimal) and hold for three to four months, or till company sufficient to slice effortlessly with a chef's knife. Once absolutely cured, those may be saved refrigerated for up to one yr however are at their nice withinside the first three months.

To serve, wipe away any extra mould with a dry fabric or towel. If you'll be the usage of best a part of a sausage, the usage of a pointy knife, rating the casing round its circumference partway from the end, then peel away the casing from the vicinity to be sliced.

SBRICIOLONA

Sbriciolona, a sort of Italian fennel salami, may be loosely translated as "crumbly thing." This full-flavored salami is made with finely floor and coarsely floor pork, which yield a completely unique texture. Traditionally, it isn't pressed and is eaten whilst it's miles nevertheless pretty younger and soft, however it's miles similarly desirable elderly longer till company.

MAKES ABOUT 7 POUNDS (3.2 KG) OR 2 LARGE SALAMI
10 pounds (four.five kg) boneless beef picnic or leg meat reduce into 1- inch (2.five cm) cubes
four.eight ounces (152 g)
quality sea salt 2 teaspoons
curing salt no. 2
⅛ teaspoon floor mace
2 teaspoons entire chile flakes
2 teaspoons floor chile flakes 1
tablespoon fennel pollen

five cloves garlic, pounded to a paste in a mortar with 1 teaspoon quality sea salt
½ cup (a hundred and twenty ml) dry purple wine
2 organized red meat caps, became interior out

Place the beef in a massive nonreactive bowl or container. To make the spice package, in a small bowl, integrate the ocean salt, curing salt, mace, entire and floor chile flakes, fennel pollen, and garlic and blend well. Mix the spice package calmly with the beef (see Basic Sausage Method), cover, and refrigerate overnight.

Refrigerate the elements of your grinder till equipped to use. Following the commands for grinding, in shape the grinder with the smallest plate and grind 1/2 of of the beef once. Stop the grinder, transfer to the most important plate, and grind the final beef once. Combine each batches of beef, pour withinside the wine, and blend through hand for approximately four minutes, till you could select out up maximum of the combinationture with each fingers with out it falling apart.

Following the commands for Casing, Linking, Looping, and Tying, case the farce withinside the red meat caps, ensuring there aren't anyt any air holes, then truss tightly with wire as you'll a roast (see How to Tie a Roast). Hang the sausages in a appropriate place at 65°F to 75°F (18°C to 21°C) for four days, till they've became a rosy hue, and preferably have a bit little bit of a white bloom of mildew. Then pass to a cooler place (50°F/10°C might be optimal) and cling for approximately four months, till the preferred firmness has been achieved. These salami will maintain for up to ten months however are great in the first four months after they're completed curing.

To serve, wipe away any extra mildew with a dry material or towel. If you may be the usage of most effective a part of a sausage, the usage of a pointy knife, rating the casing round its circumference partway from the stop, then peel away the casing from the vicinity to be sliced. Store partly reduce Sbriciolona refrigerated, with the reduce stop loosely wrapped in parchment paper.

THREE

PÂTÉS: POTTED MEATS, TERRINES & LOAVES

Pâtés, which encompass potted meats, terrines, and loaves, are essential participants of the charcutier's repertoire. They sparkle enticingly from keep home windows in Paris, offer the scrumptious makings for a picnic, and summon you to the desk to revel in a leisurely meal. These savory and addictive meaty items run the gamut from the haute and the elegant, which includes the seductive Duck Liver Mousse, to the country and the everyday, which includes the standard American-fashion Meat Loaf. They embody a huge variety of strategies as well, from the tremendously easy salt "cooked" Foie Gras Torchon to the tough four-day, multiprocessed Headcheese. In different words, each curious prepare dinner dinner and charcuterie devotee, from amateur to master, will locate some thing to pursue on this bankruptcy.

Tools of the Trade

The recipes on this bankruptcy require little unique equipment. A grinder is reachable for a few arrangements however now no longer important for all. For making terrines and loaves, a classic, 1½-quart (1.four L) square terrine mildew made from enameled forged iron with a good becoming lid is sturdy, attractive, guarantees even cooking, and could final for lots years. But in case you don't have a terrine, a bread pan or small baking dish will do in a pinch. A tamis, or drum sieve, is the important thing to a velvety-textured mousse, however a quality-mesh sieve will work. For potted meats, ramekins, canning jars, crocks, and locking-lid jars are all useful, however you could frequently be substituted for the different.

Potted Meats

Potted meats are a easy form of pâté made from cooked meats which have been shredded or chopped and certain with both fats or a gelatinous cooking broth after which set in a crock for serving or keeping. The perception of potted meats appears truly antiquated, however they're reachable to serve for hors d'oeuvres for the busy, modern host. They may be made ahead, then sealed and saved for weeks or months, in order that the subsequent time surprising visitors drop in, you could simply attain into your larder for the makings of a splendid canapé or first course.

The recipes that comply with are divided into categories: potted meats certain with fats, and potted meats certain with wealthy broth.

Potted Meats Bound with Fat

Rillettes and different potted meats certain with fats are scrumptious arrangements that may be made effortlessly when you have confits available and are really well worth the attempt even in case you don't. Simply season the beef, prepare dinner dinner it lengthy and gradual in its very own fats or in every other lipid of your choosing, after which shred and bind it with a number of its cooking juices and fats. Pack the combination right into a pot or terrine even as it's far nevertheless warm, and cowl it with a layer of fats, with a view to harden because it cools to shape an hermetic seal that protects the beef, permitting it to ripen and hold longer.

Nearly any sort of meat may be organized and preserved the usage of this method. Pork, duck, and goose are the maximum common, however rabbit, chicken, turkey, or different chicken works beautifully, as well. Season the beef an afternoon in advance as you'll for creating a confit and prepare dinner dinner it the subsequent day, once more as you'll a confit: gradual and coffee and absolutely submerged in fats. If you're cooking at the range top, your pot ought to in no way pretty attain a simmer. If the usage of the oven, a temperature round 250°F (120°C) will do the trick. Continue cooking beyond the factor you'll for a confit, till the beef slips effortlessly from the bone, or withinside the case of boneless meat, till you could pull it aside with nearly no attempt.

Once the beef is cooked, permit it to relaxation withinside the fats for 20 to 30 minutes, till cool sufficient to handle. Separate the beef from its cooking liquid and switch to a large, shallow bowl. Pour the cooking liquid right into a tall, clean box to cool. The fats will cut loose the gelée, the wealthy meaty juices that gather all through the cooking process. Ladle the fats off into every other box, and set the fats and gelée apart one after the other even as you shred or chop the beef.

In maximum cases, the great texture is completed in case you shred with the aid of using hand, despite the fact that there are instances whilst a coarser texture can be desired, wherein case you can need to cut the beef with a knife. Avoid the usage of a meals processor, as it's far all too smooth to overwork your meat and land up with an unattractive paste. The meat ought to be soft and shred effortlessly. Discard any bones, skin, gristle, or cartilage. When the beef is uniformly shredded in your liking, fold in approximately 1/2 of of the gelée and a number of the fats with the aid of using hand. How a whole lot fats and liquid you upload will rely upon the sort of meat, the water content material of the fats, and a number of different factors, which includes your very own preferences.

> ## TASTING FOR SEASONING
> When sampling charcuterie before cooking, it is important to taste it at the temperature at which it will be served. Cold food needs to be more highly seasoned, whereas food that will be served hot needs less seasoning.

Working fats-certain meats is a touch like operating bread dough. The
movement of your fingers facilitates to make a cohesive meat mass. Incorporating the fats slowly offers the beef time to take in it and could bring about a creamier texture. Use your palms just like the tines of a fork to paintings withinside the fats. Try now no longer to mash the beef; the ensuing combination ought to experience mild and unfastened as opposed to pasty. When the combination feels silky and as aleven though it can't maintain any extra fats, pause for a bit. If the combination dries out at the floor and edges after some minutes, take into account including extra fats. But if small swimming pools of fats start to shape at the floor, you've got got reached the factor of perfection.

Add freshly chopped herbs together with thyme, oregano, chives, flat-leaf parsley, or rosemary at the side of wine, brandy, or different flavorings.

Now flavor for seasoning. Fat-certain potted meats are normally served particularly cool. Cooler temperatures mute the flavors, so that you will need it to flavor enormously pro even as it's far nevertheless warm. If it desires a touch swagger, you could upload extra of the gelée, a pinch extra of the seasoning spices, or extra salt.

Traditionally, potted meats certain with fats have been sealed below a layer in their cooking fats for longer keeping. Although you could devour them proper away, sealing and storing them lets in them to ripen particularly and broaden flavor. Pack or pot the meats into clean, glass jars with lids (locking-lid glass jars are best for this task) or a ceramic crock or terrine with a geared up lid, urgent the beef in as you visit cast off any air pockets. Chill for 1 hour withinside the fridge, then pour roomtemperature cooking fats on top, developing a layer ½ inch (12 mm) thick. Cover and refrigerate. After some hours, test the fats seal. Fat will occasionally retain to seep into the beef because it settles. If any of the beef is poking up or seen thru the fats, pour every other skinny layer of liquid fats on top. Well sealed and refrigerated, potted meats will hold withinside the fridge for numerous months.

To serve, put off the jar or crock from the fridge and permit it To heat to room temperature. The pinnacle layer of fats may be scraped off and reused to reseal any leftovers, repurposed for cooking, or, in a classically decadent fashion, stirred into the beef and savored.

VARIATIONS ON POTTED MEATS BOUND WITH FAT

Once you analyze the primary technique for making potted meats sure with fats, you may attempt making such a tasty variations.

Duck Rillettes: Make with entire duck or duck legs simmered in rendered duck fats and pro with quatre épices, thyme, and dry sherry.

Guinea Hen Rillettes: Make with entire guinea fowl or guinea fowl legs simmered in rendered duck or bird fats and pro with clean summer time season savory, white wine, and roasted peppercorns.

Goose Rillettes with Black Truffle: Simmer goose legs and wing joints in rendered goose fats or duck fats and season with overwhelmed garlic, Cognac, and grated clean black truffle. Garnish character crocks with a shaving of black truffle.

Smoked Potted Pork: Use a aggregate of slab bacon and boneless red meat shoulder simmered in lard and end with a touch of bourbon.

RABBIT RILLETTES

For maximum potted meats sure with fats, consisting of the

ones made with red meat or poultry, we favor to prepare dinner dinner meat at the bone—however rabbit is complete of tiny bones that may be clean to miss whilst you are shredding the beef. For this recipe, bone the rabbit and shop the carcass for creating a flavorful broth.

MAKES 6 TO EIGHT CUPS (1.4TO 2 L)
1 rabbit, three to four pounds (1.four to 1.eight kg)
1 teaspoon peppercorns
three allspice berries
1 entire clove
1 juniper berry
2 tablespoons (1.2 ounces/34 g) great sea salt 2 cloves garlic, smashed
1 dried bay leaf
¼ cup (60 ml) Madeira
eight cups (2 L) rendered duck fats or lard, or a aggregate
¼ cup (15 g) finely chopped clean sage

Remove the heart, liver, and kidneys from the rabbit and reserve for Marsha's Grilled Rabbit Spiedini with Chicories, Olives, and Almonds. Following the commands for Boned Rabbit, bone all the rabbit besides for the forelegs and vicinity the beef and forelegs in a bowl.

In a spice grinder, integrate the peppercorns, allspice, clove, and juniper and grind finely. Transfer to a small bowl, upload the salt, garlic, bay, and Madeira, and stir to mix. Add the spice combination to the rabbit and blend to coat evenly. Cover and refrigerate overnight.

Preheat the oven to 250°F (one hundred twenty°C). Place the rabbit in a tall, slender ovenproof pot and cowl with the fats. Warm over low warmness at the range pinnacle for approximately 10 minutes, till the fats has simply melted, then switch the pot to the oven to prepare dinner dinner slowly for two to a few hours, stirring lightly each 30 minutes. To take a look at for doneness, dispose of one of the rabbit forelegs and pull a number of the beef from the bone. It ought to yield completely, leaving the bone pretty easy. Once you've got got decided the beef is done, dispose of the pot from the oven, pull the beef off the opposite foreleg, discard the bones, and go back all of the beef to the pot.

Let the beef cool for approximately 20 minutes, then the usage of a slotted spoon, switch the rabbit meat to a bowl. Strain the fats via a great-mesh sieve right into a tall, clean container. Let stand for approximately 20 minutes, till the fats separates from the gelée. Ladle off the fats into its personal container, and set the gelée and fats apart separately.

Shred the beef with the aid of using hand, then paintings withinside the gelée and the fats, approximately
½ cup (one hundred twenty ml) at a time, alternating among gelée and fats with every addition. When the rillettes sense creamy, loose, and can not soak up any

extra of the fats (search for small swimming pools of fats at the floor of the beef), take a look at for seasoning. Refrigerate a pattern of the rillettes for 15 minutes. Evaluate the flavor and texture and regulate the seasonings if necessary. If the rillettes appear grainy or dry, upload extra fats. Fold the sage into the rillettes.

Pack or pot the rillettes into easy glass jars, ceramic crocks, or a terrine, leaving a ½-inch (12 mm) head space. Chill for 1 hour withinside the refrigerator, then pour a number of the room-temperature cooking fats on pinnacle, growing a layer ½ inch (12 mm) thick. After 1 hour, test the fats seal following the commands, then cowl and refrigerate.

If the rillettes are nicely sealed, they'll hold nicely for numerous months. The taste will virtually enhance after the primary week. Any greater cooking fats may be strained and refrigerated for numerous months to be reused for any other batch of rillettes or different low-temperature cooking, consisting of confits.

CICCIOLI

Ciccioli is a conventional Italian instruction concocted from all the piggy bits, scraps of meat, fats, and pores and skin, leftover from hog butchering. But there may be little consensus as to the technique and seasoning used to put together ciccioli, and there appear to be as many recipes for ciccioli as there are picturesque, red meat- adoring villages in Italy. This model is a highly spiced, chunky, but spreadable pâté organized in addition to rillettes however with a coarser texture and the introduced gain of red meat crackling. Any leftover highly spiced lard may be reused numerous instances and is incredible for cooking. Try the usage of it in location of normal lard for a devilish model of the ChickenFried Quail.

MAKES ABOUT EIGHT CUPS (2 L)
3½ pounds (1.6 kg) boneless pores and skin-on red meat shoulder, in a unmarried piece
1 tablespoon plus 2 teaspoons (1.2 ounces/34g) high-quality sea salt 1½ teaspoons freshly floor pepper
1 tablespoon entire chile flakes
1 head garlic, cloves separated, peeled, and overwhelmed 12 cups (2.eight L) lard
2 teaspoons finely floor chile flakes ¼ cup (60 ml) dry white wine

Skin the red meat shoulder (see Skinning the Pig) and set apart the beef. Using the top of a pointy knife and a mild touch, rating the floor of the pores and skin, making straight, strains spaced approximately 1 inch (2.five cm) apart.

Cut the shoulder meat into 1-inch (2.five cm) cubes and location in a massive bowl. Season with the salt, pepper, entire chile flakes, and garlic, coating the beef evenly. Cover and refrigerate overnight.

The subsequent day, preheat the oven to 400°F (200°C). Outfit a roasting pan with a rack.

In a massive, heavy braiser, soften the lard over low heat. Rub the pores and skin of the shoulder with 1 teaspoon of the melted lard and set the pores and skin, fats facet down, at the rack and location withinside the oven. Cook for approximately 30 minutes, till the pores and skin turns golden brown. Turn down the oven temperature to 275°F (135°C) and maintain cooking for 1 to 1½ hours longer, till crisp and brittle. Remove from the oven and permit cool. Pour any collected fats from the roasting pan into the pot of lard.

Add the pro red meat shoulder and its marinade to the pot of melted fats and location over very low heat. Cook for approximately three hours, ensuring the pot by no means reaches a simmer. The meat is prepared whilst it may be cut up without difficulty with a fork. Remove the pot from the warmth and permit relaxation for 20 minutes.

Using a slotted spoon, switch the beef to a massive bowl. Strain the fats via a high-quality-mesh sieve right into a tall, clean box. Remarry any solids stuck withinside the sieve, together with spices or bits of meat or garlic, with the red meat. Let the fats stand for approximately 20 minutes, till the fats separates from the gelée, then ladle off the fats into its personal box and set the gelée and fats apart separately.

Pour ½ cup (one hundred twenty ml) of the fats and ½ cup (one hundred twenty ml) of the gelée into the bowl of red meat. Coarsely shred the beef via way of means of hand even as operating withinside the liquid, then blend withinside the floor chile flakes and wine. Break the cooked pores and skin into more or less ½-inch (12 mm) pieces, both via way of means of hand or with a knife, and fold into the shredded red meat. Then upload every other ½

cup (one hundred twenty ml) of the fats and ½ cup (one hundred twenty ml) of the gelée. Refrigerate a pattern of the combination for 15 minutes. Evaluate the flavor and texture and alter the seasonings if necessary. If the combination appears grainy or dry, upload extra fats.

Pack or pot the combination into easy glass jars, ceramic crocks, or a terrine, leaving a ½-inch (12 mm) area among the pinnacle of the beef and the lip of the vessel. Chill for 1 hour withinside the refrigerator, then pour a number of the room-temperature cooking fats on pinnacle, developing a layer ½ inch (12 mm) thick. After 1 hour, take a look at the fats seal following the commands then cowl and refrigerate.

If the ciccioli is nicely sealed, it'll live accurate for numerous months. The taste will simply enhance after the primary week. Any greater cooking fats may be strained and refrigerated for numerous months to be reused for every other batch of ciccioli or repurposed for cooking.

Potted Meats Bound with Rich Broth

Potted meats certain with wealthy broth are a alternatively unique concoction, extra comparable to a delicious, wealthy meaty braise eaten cold. Although the seasoning, sluggish cooking, shredding, and potting system is much like potted meats certain with fat, those potted meats draw their soul electricity from their flavorful, gelatinous cooking liquid. The pro meat is cooked till very smooth, then shredded or chopped, certain with broth, packed in a terrine, and chilled to solidify ensuing in a mosaic of meat and seasonings suspended in a flavorful, herbal gelatin.

For the excellent potted meats certain with broth, pick stewing or braising cuts from flavorful, well-advanced muscles, ideally at the bone. Nearly any meat may be organized on this fashion, however the ones tougher, bonier cuts that comprise the maximum gelatin, including beef, veal, lamb, or beef shanks, shoulders, heads, and cheeks, will yield the excellent consequences. The addition of a cut up pig trotter or calf foot will deliver the cooking liquor a exquisite quantity of herbal gelatin with a purpose to act as a binder.

Season your meat beforehand as you'll for a braise. Brining the meats in advance of cooking is sometimes recommended for mainly dense or bony cuts, including beef trotters or head. Simmer the meats lightly in a flavorful meat broth with aromatics till very smooth or till the beef slips without difficulty from the bone. Allow the meats to chill to room temperature of their cooking liquid. Drain the meats, booking the liquor, and switch the meats to a large, shallow bowl. Discard any bones and aromatics.

Return the braising liquor to a saucepan and decrease with the aid of using approximately 1/2 of. Test the efficiency of the gelatin withinside the liquid with the aid of using ladling liquor to a intensity of ½ inch (12 mm) right into a ramekin or shallow bowl, then region withinside the fridge for approximately 20 minutes. If it's far corporation whilst chilled, then the liquor has good enough gelatin. If it's far nevertheless liquid or holds collectively loosely, maintain to lessen the liquor to pay attention the gelatin. Be certain to flavor because it reduces, because the salts and seasonings will listen because the liquid evaporates. If it starts offevolved to appear overly pro, forestall decreasing irrespective of the consequences of the gelatin test. It is higher to have a loosely certain potted meat than an excessively salted one. Allow the completed liquor to chill to room temperature. (Note: Some chefs like to feature business gelatin as an coverage coverage or shortcut. Commercial gelatin, frequently of doubtful origins, is commonly needless for potted meats, supplying you operate a enough quantity of meat and right broth and make an effort to lessen the cooking liquor.)

When it's far cool sufficient to handle, shred or chop the beef, discarding any bone, skin, or sinew. Add any herbs and/or garnishes. Ladle in small quantities of the braising liquor to moisten and blend lightly with the aid of using hand. You want to feature simply sufficient liquid to bind the beef. Refrigerate 1 tablespoon of the aggregate for 30 minutes. Evaluate the cohesiveness and the flavor and alter the seasonings if necessary.

Pot your meat in glass jars, crocks, or terrines. If you intend on turning out your potted meat (that is, now no longer serving it withinside the vessel it changed into saved in), you'll need to line the terrine or different vessel with plastic wrap, permitting it to overhang the perimeters with the aid of using as a minimum 2 inches (five cm). If you'll be serving your potted meat en terrine, you may bypass this step. Either way, ladle a small quantity of the cooking liquid into the terrine or different vessel, sufficient to coat the lowest to a intensity of approximately ½ inch

(12 mm). You will want approximately ½ cup (a hundred and twenty ml). Follow with a layer of approximately 1/2 of of the beef. Press the beef down lightly. Cover with a bit extra liquid (once more approximately ½ cup/a hundred and twenty ml), observed with the aid of using the the rest of the beef. Press lightly once more, after which pinnacle with a bit extra liquid to cover (approximately 1 cup/240 ml). You will not often want all the cooking liquid to set your potted meat, and the the rest may be stored for making soups or sauces. Cover the vessel (when you have coated the terrine with plastic wrap, deliver the overhang as much as cover) and refrigerate in a single day to set the potted meat earlier than serving.

To flip out a terrine, dispose of it from the fridge and invert it onto a slicing board, then cautiously raise off the vessel. (Do now no longer carry the potted meat to room temperature earlier than you unmold it.) Carefully peel away the plastic wrap, then slice the potted meat. If you may be serving the slices later, switch them to a baking sheet covered with parchment paper and go back to the fridge till serving time. If you're serving the potted meat en terrine, simply insert a spoon and enjoy.

VARIATIONS ON POTTED MEATS BOUND WITH RICH BROTH

Jambon Persille: A Parisian classic! Simmer a whole brined ham, 1 yellow onion, and a few split pig trotters until quite tender. Shred the meat and season with chopped capers, cornichons, tarragon, and shallots; a splash of white wine vinegar or champagne vinegar; and lots of chopped fresh parsley, *bien sur*!

Pork Cheek Terrine: Brown pork cheeks and then braise in a rich pork broth seasoned with chile flakes, minced yellow onion, chopped garlic, and fresh rosemary, savory, and thyme. Leave the cheeks whole, set them in a rectangular terrine, chill, and slice to serve.

OXTAIL TERRINE

The bony, crosscut queue de boeuf (French for "oxtail") is teeming with earthy taste and with gelatin, that is the important thing to the fulfillment of this terrine. Top slices with a robust mustardcaper sauce and serve along a handful of highly spiced cress.

MAKES 6 TO EIGHT CUPS (I.FOUR TO 2 L) OR ONE THREE-POUND (I.FOUR KG) TERRINE
five pounds (2.three kg) oxtails, reduce crosswise into portions 2 inches (five cm) thick
Fine sea salt
2 tablespoons lard

2 cups (480 ml) dry purple wine
2 cups (480 g) entire canned tomatoes with their juice
1 pig trotter, split
1 yellow onion, quartered
2 carrots, peeled and sliced at the diagonal
1 inch (2.five cm) thick
five cloves garlic, peeled however
left entire 1 dried bay leaf
½ teaspoon peppercorns
1 teaspoon piment d'Espelette
½ cup (30 g) chopped clean flat-leaf parsley

Rinse the oxtails below cool strolling water and pat dry. Place in a massive bowl and season liberally with salt. Cover and refrigerate in a single day.

The subsequent day, in a massive, heavy sauté pan, soften the lard over medium-excessive warmness. Add the oxtails in a single, uncrowded layer and brown nicely on all sides. Using a slotted spoon, switch the oxtails to a massive braiser. Pour the wine into the sauté pan and deglaze over medium warmness, stirring with a timber spoon to loosen the fond from the lowest of the pan. Pour the wine over the oxtails, then upload the tomatoes, pig's foot, onion, carrots, garlic, bay leaf, and peppercorns.

Add water simply to cowl the oxtails and 1 teaspoon salt and convey to a boil. Lower the warmth to a lazy simmer and read off any particulates that upward thrust to the surface. Continue to simmer, uncovered, for three hours.

When each the oxtails and the foot are fork-tender, the use of a slotted spoon, switch them to a platter. Line a colander with cheesecloth (or use a chinois or different pleasant-mesh sieve) and stress the broth via the colander right into a stockpot. Place the pot over medium warmness and prepare dinner dinner till decreased via way of means of approximately one-fourth. Ladle the broth to a intensity of ½ inch (12 mm) right into a ramekin and refrigerate for approximately 20 minutes. If it's miles corporation and gelatinous whilst chilled, it's miles ready. If it's miles nonetheless a hint runny, lessen in addition and check again. Taste for seasoning and alter if necessary.

Pull all of the beef off of the oxtails and the foot, discarding the pores and skin and bones. Toss the beef with the piment d'Espelette and parsley.

Following the commands for Potted Meats Bound with Rich Broth, pot the beef in glass jars, crocks, or a terrine, lining the terrine with plastic wrap in case you plan on turning out the potted meat to serve, then refrigerate and function directed.

Headcheese

HEADCHEESE

Admittedly, Headcheese isn't for everyone. But it does have its devotees, and we see increasingly humans transformed all of the time. At the Fatted Calf, we make a batch of headcheese approximately as soon as each six weeks, and whilst it's miles long past, it's miles long past till we've gathered sufficient red meat heads to make any other batch. The headcheese lovers generally tend to pine loudly in its absence. Headcheese, aleven though now no longer difficult, is a time-eating exertions of love. This model takes 4 days from begin to finish. On the

first day, you are making brine for the heads, you then definately brine the heads the subsequent day. This is accompanied via way of means of an afternoon of cooking, chopping, and putting the terrine. The terrine chills in a single day till subsequently you are making a wish, flip out your terrine, and if the celebs have aligned, you've got got a mosaic of head meat of your personal making that slices beautifully—till it's miles long past. Serve with baguette, cornichons, olives, and mustard, or provide as a part of a salad path with highly spiced cress dressed with a smelly vinaigrette.

MAKES ABOUT THREE QUARTS (2.EIGHT L) OR TWO THREE-POUND (I.FOUR KG) TERRINES HEAD BRINE

I tablespoon peppercorns
I tablespoon fennel seeds
I juniper berry
I dried bay leaf
I pound (450 g) pleasant sea
salt 12 ounces (340 g) sugar
7 quarts (6.6 L) boiling water
2 teaspoons curing salt no. I

MEATS

I pores and skin-on pig head, cut up or
quartered and mind removed
three pig trotters, cut up
2 pounds (900 g) bone-in, pores and skin-on beef shoulder, in
a unmarried piece

GARNISH

I tablespoon fennel pollen
2 teaspoons chile flakes

1 teaspoon freshly floor pepper
⅛ teaspoon floor mace
   Grated zest and juice of one lemon
¼ cup (60 ml) dry white wine
¼ cup (15 g) chopped sparkling flat-leaf parsley

On day 1, make the brine. Place the peppercorns, fennel seeds, juniper berry, and bay leaf on a rectangular of cheesecloth, deliver the corners together, and tie securely with cord to make a sachet (or use a muslin bag). Measure the ocean salt and sugar right into a 5-gallon (19 L) nonreactive bucket and toss withinside the sachet. Pour withinside the boiling water and stir to dissolve the salt and sugar. Let cool to room temperature overnight.

On day 2, stir the curing salt into the brine. Add the pinnacle, trotters, and shoulder to the brine and pinnacle them with a plate to preserve them submerged. Refrigerate for twenty-four hours.

On day three, drain the meats right into a massive colander, discarding the brine and sachet. Rinse the meats gently beneathneath cool jogging water and pat dry, then placed them in a tall, slender pot. Add water to cover, region over excessive warmth, and produce to a boil. Lower the warmth to a energetic simmer and browse any impurities that upward push to the surface. Cook, exposed, for three hours, then take a look at the pinnacle for tenderness. The meat need to start to shy away from the bone and the ears need to be softened.

Carefully put off the meats to a tray to cool. Line a colander with cheesecloth (or use a chinois or different fine-mesh sieve) and pressure the broth thru the colander right into a stockpot. Place the pot over medium warmth and prepare dinner dinner till decreased through approximately half. Ladle the broth to a intensity of ½ inch (12 mm) right into a ramekin and refrigerate for approximately 20 minutes. If it's far corporation and gelatinous while chilled, it's far ready. If it's far nonetheless a hint runny, lessen similarly and take a look at again. Taste for seasoning and regulate if necessary.

Pull the beef from the bones of the pinnacle and trotters. Discard the bones. Slice the ears and the trotter pores and skin into strips ¼ inch (6 mm) wide. Tear the cheek meat through hand into portions of approximately the equal size, and reduce all the closing head meat and the beef shoulder into ½-inch (12 mm) cubes. Place all of the beef in a massive bowl and upload the fennel pollen, chile flakes, pepper, mace, lemon zest and juice, wine, and parsley. Mix gingerly to comprise the garnish.

Following the commands for Potted Meats Bound with Rich Broth, pot the beef in glass jars, crocks, or 2 terrines, lining the terrines with plastic wrap in case you plan on turning out the potted meat to serve, then refrigerate overnight. On day 4, function directed.

Baked Terrines and Loaves

A terrine is a kind of pâté or forcemeat this is baked in a mold, additionally known as a terrine. A loaf is a forcemeat this is mounded and fashioned through hand and baked exposed to shape a crust. Both are made with pro meats which can be floor and blended with a binder to assist preserve their shape, and each are typically garnished with herbs, vegetables, or different uncooked or cooked meats earlier than they're baked in a low oven. The handiest distinction is the dish or its absence.

Terrines and loaves may be crafted from maximum any meat or chicken however normally include a few beef to assist to enhance the feel and fats content. Ideally, a loaf or terrine consists of approximately 30 percentage fats. Many conventional terrines and loaves include organ meats including liver or gizzard, further to meat and fats, however it's far a not unusualplace false impression that they constantly include those or are specifically made out of them. If you don't take care of organ meats, you want now no longer upload them. But if you could attain good-first-rate sparkling organ meats, we urge you to attempt cooking with them, as they upload a diffused intensity to the taste of many preparations.

Marinate the meats an afternoon beforehand as you will for maximum sausage.

Prior to grinding the beef, put together any garniture to feature after the beef is floor. Confit of duck gizzard, olives, brandied fruits, poached tongues, diced liver, braised shallots, chopped herbs, cooked mushrooms, strips of lean meat, and the like several make appealing and (delicious) garnishes.

Grind the beef as you'll for sausage. Rustic country-fashion terrines and loaves are typically floor handiest as soon as. But for finer, lightertextured terrines, you may grind the beef twice. After the beef is floor, fold to your panade or different binder in addition to any garnish to be incorporated. In a few cases, the garnish is artfully organized to create a mosaic in every slice. Reserve those garnishes till the terrine is assembled.

If you're making a meat loaf or rustic pâté loaf that you may form through hand, line a baking sheet with parchment paper, blend the beef well, switch it to the organized baking sheet, and mould into the favored form. Smooth the rims together along with your arms to create a seamless,

uniform floor to save you cracking at some point of baking. Refrigerate the loaf for at the least half-hour earlier than baking to assist to save you fats loss at some point of cooking. When the loaf is chilled, put off the parchment-coated pan from the fridge and area immediately in a preheated 300°F (150°C) oven. Bake till a thermometer inserted into the middle of the loaf registers 140°F (60°C). Loaves may be served heat, room temperature, or chilled as favored, usually permitting the loaf to relaxation for at the least 10 mins earlier than slicing.

If the pâté is to be cooked en terrine, you may want to line the terrine (see Four Ways to Line a Terrine) earlier than you upload the forcemeat.

Lining the vessel permits for smooth unmolding as soon as the terrine is cooked. Add your meat in increments to the coated terrine, urgent firmly after every addition. If you're arranging garnish withinside the terrine, area it among layers of meat or down the middle of the terrine. Pack the farce to the lip of the terrine, and fold over the extra lining to cowl the beef. If you've got got any uncovered meat reduce an additional piece of anything lining you're the use of or a bit lower back fats for a patch job. If you land up with an excessive amount of lining, trim it with scissors to reduce overlap. Keep in thoughts a bit overlap is fine, because the lining will recede barely at some point of cooking. Lid the terrine.

Baking and Unmolding

Baking a terrine in a water bath helps to ensure even cooking. Fold a kitchen towel in half and place in the bottom of a roasting pan to act as a buffer. Place the loaded terrine on top. Pour simmering water into the pan to reach one-third of the way up the sides of the terrine. Carefully place the roasting pan in a preheated 300°F (150°C) oven.

If your terrine has a small hole in its lid, make sure the side with the hole is placed closest to the oven door to simplify taking the temperature of the terrine during cooking. Cook to an internal temperature of 140°F (60°C). Gently lift the terrine from the water bath and let cool to room temperature before refrigerating.

Pressing is a way this is once in a while used to compress the terrine in order that it could be sliced thinly with out crumbling, aleven though it also includes now no longer vital If the terrine is packed cautiously previous to baking. It is most advantageous to keep away from urgent, however, due to the fact urgent a terrine leaches out the scrumptious cooking juices that assist to preserve it moist. If

you want to press a terrine, you have to use a weight this is suited for your terrine mould. A block of timber reduce to length and wrapped in plastic wrap works well. Place the block immediately on pinnacle of the still-heat terrine after which area the lid on pinnacle of the block.

To unmold your chilled terrine, discover and area the terrine in a hot-water tubtub for approximately 30 seconds to soften the fats lightly at the outside and unfasten the edges and backside from the vessel. Remove from the water tubtub and invert onto a slicing board. If the terrine does now no longer slip without difficulty from the mould, flip it upright, loosen it lightly on both quit with a rubber spatula, after which invert again.

Slice as a whole lot of the terrine as you intend on serving. The terrine lining, whether or not it's far caul fats, belly, lower back fats, or skin, is absolutely edible.

If you don't plan on serving the terrine proper away, you may shop it refrigerated in its mould for approximately a week. If you intend on retaining your terrine longer, you may cap it with duck or beef fats, just like a confit (see Basic Confit Making). Before capping it, put off any gelée that has fashioned withinside the backside or on the edges of the terrine.

FOUR WAYS TO LINE A TERRINE
Caul fats: Versatile caul fats is the only manner to line a

terrine and may be reduce to healthy any length mold. It is skinny and transparent, presenting a peek at the beef within, but sturdy. Lay a huge piece to your terrine, permitting it to overhang the perimeters with the aid of using approximately three inches (7.five cm).

Back fats: Strips of thinly sliced again fats makes an impressive-searching all-white lining for a terrine. Slice the again fats on a meat slicer, then layer in the terrine, barely overlapping every slice.

Belly: Pork stomach or thinly sliced bacon makes a flavorful, streaky lining for a terrine. When the use of bacon, hold in thoughts that it'll upload to the seasoning of the terrine. Be certain to overlap the slices, as there's a small quantity of shrinkage for the duration of cooking.

Duck pores and skin: If you're the use of an entire duck to make the forcemeat, you may use the pores and skin to line the terrine. You will want to observe the commands for Whole Boned Bird, then separate the beef and pores and skin with out tearing the pores and skin. With a knife, scrape away any extra fats or glands which might be connected to the pores and skin. Lay the sheet of pores and skin withinside the terrine, urgent it into the corners.

From front: stomach, caul fats, again fats, duck pores and skin

MEAT LOAF

Meat Loaf

This traditional American pâté is formed right into a huge oval loaf and glazed with tangy cocktail sauce. A thick slice of this meat loaf over creamy mashed potatoes is a component of beauty. Any leftovers make exquisite sandwiches with complete-grain mustard and Pickled Red Onion Rings.

MAKES ONE 3½-POUND (1.6 KG) LOAF;
SERVES 6 TO 8
FORCEMEAT
¾ teaspoon peppercorns

2 allspice berries

2 teaspoons fennel seeds

1 teaspoon chile flakes

1 complete clove

1¼ pounds (570 g) boneless lean pork from eye of spherical or sirloin, reduce into 1-inch (2.five cm) cubes

1 pound (450 g) boneless red meat picnic, reduce into 1-inch (2.five cm) cubes

four ounces (one hundred fifteen g) red meat again fats, reduce into 1inch (2.five cm) cubes 1 tablespoon best sea salt

2 teaspoons chopped garlic

four ounces (one hundred fifteen g) bacon, chopped

    PANADE

2 cups (three hundred g) diced

yellow onion 2 tablespoons

unsalted butter

¼ teaspoon best sea salt

6 tablespoons (22 g) clean bread crumbs

1 egg, gently beaten

½ cup (a hundred and twenty g) ketchup

1½ teaspoons Tabasco sauce

1¼ teaspoons Worcestershire sauce

1 teaspoon grated clean horseradish

¼ cup (15 g) chopped clean flat-leaf parsley

2 tablespoons chopped clean oregano

1 tablespoon chopped clean sage

1 tablespoon chopped clean thyme

    COCKTAIL SAUCE

¼ cup (60 g) ketchup

¼ teaspoon best sea salt

¼ teaspoon freshly floor pepper 1½

teaspoons grated horseradish

½ teaspoon Worcestershire sauce

½ teaspoon Tabasco sauce

Preheat the oven to 325°F (165°C). To make the forcemeat, unfold the peppercorns and allspice on a baking sheet and toast for three to five minutes, till fragrant. Let cool completely. Toast the fennel seeds the equal manner, then allow cool completely. Reserve 1/2 of of the toasted fennel seeds and 1/2 of of the chile flakes. In a spice grinder, integrate the final chile flakes and fennel seeds, the toasted peppercorns and allspice, and the clove and grind finely.

Place the red meat, pork, and fats in a huge nonreactive bowl. To make the spice package, in a small bowl, integrate the freshly floor spices, the salt, and the garlic and stir well. Mix the spice package lightly with the beef, cover, and refrigerate overnight. Reserve the bacon withinside the refrigerator. To make the panade, integrate the onions and butter in a sauté pan set over low heat. Season with the salt and sweat the onions slowly for approximately 20 minutes, till they're smooth and translucent. Transfer to a bowl and allow cool to room temperature. Add the bread crumbs, egg, ketchup, Tabasco, Worcestershire sauce, parsley, oregano, sage, and thyme to the onion and blend well. (The panade may be made an afternoon beforehand and refrigerated or simply previous to grinding the beef.)

To make the cocktail sauce, in a small bowl, integrate the ketchup, salt, pepper, horseradish, Worcestershire sauce, and Tabasco and blend well. (The sauce may be made an afternoon beforehand and refrigerated or simply previous to grinding.)

Preheat the oven to three hundred°F (150°C).

Line a baking sheet with parchment paper. Following the commands for grinding, match the grinder with the most important plate and grind the bacon once. Stop the grinder, transfer to the medium plate, and grind the red meat and red meat once. Mix the floor bacon into the floor red meat and red meat. Pour the panade over the beef and blend via way of means of hand for two to a few mins, till the farce comes collectively in a cohesive mass. Cook a small pattern of the aggregate in a sauté pan and regulate the seasonings if necessary.

Transfer the farce to the organized baking sheet. Using your hands, mould right into a long, even loaf approximately 2½ inches (6 cm) tall and 7½ inches (19 cm) wide. Smooth over any cracks in order that the floor appears

pretty uniform. If the loaf appears in any respect crumbly, go back it to the bowl to knead similarly after which reshape. Small cracks turns into larger all through cooking, making the loaf unattractive and tough to slice, so it's far crucial to ensure that it's far firmly held collectively at this point.

Using the threshold of a spatula or the again of a chef's knife, rating the pinnacle of the loaf in a diamond pattern: Facing the loaf lengthwise, flip your spatula or knife at a 45-diploma perspective and make a reduce ⅛ inch (three mm) deep from the left facet all of the manner to the proper facet. Repeat at 1- inch (2.five cm) intervals, then opposite and rating withinside the contrary direction.

Bake for 15 mins, then rotate the pan a hundred and eighty stages to make sure even cooking. Check the temperature after any other 10 mins. When a thermometer inserted into the middle of the loaf registers 100°F (38°C), get rid of the loaf from the oven and unfold the cocktail sauce lightly over the pinnacle and aspects with a spoon. Return the loaf to the oven and preserve baking for 10 to fifteen mins, till the loaf reaches an inner temperature of one hundred forty°F (60°C).

Let the loaf relaxation for as a minimum 10 mins earlier than slicing. Wrapped tightly and refrigerated, the loaf will maintain for three to four days.

FORAGER'S TERRINE

Foraging for wild mushrooms is a favourite pastime, specifically in winter, whilst the Northern California coastal woodlands are flush with golden chanterelles, black trumpets, yellow feet, and hedgehogs, that may all discover their manner into this bacon-flecked terrine. The mushroom duxelles used to taste and garnish this terrine may be made with something wild mushrooms are available. While clean wild mushrooms are preferred, dried porcini or morels paintings well, too.

MAKES ONE THREE-POUND (I.FOUR KG)
   TERRINE FORCEMEAT
five shallots, finely minced
2 tablespoons unsalted butter
6 ounces (a hundred and seventy g) red meat liver, trimmed and reduce into I-inch (2.five cm) cubes

2 cups (480 ml) complete milk

1¾ pounds (800 g) boneless red meat shoulder, reduce into 1-inch (2.five cm) cubes

14 ounces (four hundred g) red meat again fats, reduce into 1inch (2.five cm) cubes

½ teaspoon peppercorns

¼ teaspoon yellow mustard seeds

1 dried bay leaf

2 allspice berries

1 tablespoon plus 1½ teaspoons pleasant sea salt

¼ teaspoon floor ginger

¼ teaspoon piment d'Espelette or floor cayenne

⅛ teaspoon freshly grated nutmeg

PANADE

½ cup (one hundred twenty ml) meat broth, any kind (see **Basic Rich Broth**)

½ cup (one hundred twenty ml) heavy cream

½ cup (30 g) clean bread crumbs

GARNISH

1 cup (163 g) The Charcutier's Wild Mushroom Duxelles

2 tablespoons Madeira

1 cup (one hundred forty g) finely diced bacon, home made or store-sold 2 tablespoons chopped clean thyme, plus three sprigs

2 tablespoons chopped clean flat-leaf parsley

2 tablespoons chopped clean sage, plus three complete leaves 1 piece caul fats or sliced red meat fats again, approximately

eight via way of means of 20 inches (20 via way of means of 50 cm)

To make the forcemeat, integrate the shallots and butter in a sauté pan set over low warmness and sweat slowly for approximately 20 mins, till smooth and translucent. Remove from the warmth and permit cool to room temperature.

In a bowl, integrate the liver and the milk, immersing the liver fully. Cover and refrigerate.

Place the red meat and again fats in a huge nonreactive bowl. To make the spice package, in a spice grinder, integrate the peppercorns, mustard seeds,

bay, and allspice and grind finely. Transfer to a small bowl, upload the salt, ginger, piment d'Espelette, and nutmeg. Mix the shallots and the spice package with the beef, cover, and refrigerate overnight.

To make the panade, in a small bowl, integrate the broth, cream, and bread crumbs and blend well. Set aside.

Drain the red meat liver, discarding the milk, and upload to the marinated meat in conjunction with ¼ cup (forty one g) of the mushroom duxelles. Follow the commands for grinding, match the grinder with the smallest plate and grind finely twice. Fold the panade and Madeira withinside the floor meat till absolutely incorporated, then upload the final duxelles, bacon, and the chopped thyme, parsley, and sage. Cook a small pattern of the combination in a sauté pan, then sit back the pattern, flavor for seasonings, and alter if necessary.

Preheat the oven to 325°F (165°C). Bring a kettle full of water to a simmer. Line a terrine with the caul fats. Arrange the sage leaves and thyme sprigs alongside the middle of the terrine after which fill the terrine with the farce. Pack the farce properly, tamping down after every addition, after which tapping the terrine in opposition to the paintings floor to launch any air pockets. The farce ought to be degree with the lip of the terrine. Fold the extra caul fats over the top; trim any overlap and lid the terrine.

Fold a kitchen towel in half and place in the bottom of a roasting pan large enough to accommodate the terrine. Set the loaded terrine on the towel. Pour the simmering water into the roasting pan to reach one-third of the way up the sides of the terrine. Carefully place in the oven and bake for about 1 hour, until a thermometer inserted into the center of the terrine registers 140°F (60°C). Remove the roasting pan from the oven and gently lift the terrine from the water bath. Let cool to room temperature, then refrigerate overnight.

To unmold the terrine, discover and vicinity the terrine in a hot-water tubtub for approximately 30 seconds to soften the fats lightly at the outdoors and unfasten the lowest and aspects from the mold. Remove from the water tubtub, invert onto a reducing board, and raise off the mold. Slice as a great deal as you intend on serving, then wrap the the rest properly and shop withinside the fridge for up to one week.

Spiced Lamb Terrine

SPICED LAMB TERRINE

Lamb aficionados pride on this boldly spiced terrine with chunks of poached lamb tongue and entire coriander seeds. Serve slices of the terrine with grilled flatbread and quince chutney as a part of a North African–stimulated meal.

**MAKES ONE THREE-POUND (I.FOUR KG)
TERRINE FORCEMEAT**

I ½ teaspoons peppercorns

2 teaspoons cumin seeds

2 allspice berries

2 dried bay leaves

2 pounds (900 g) boneless lean lamb shank, reduce into 1-inch (2.five cm) cubes

1 pound (450 g) red meat again fats, reduce into 1inch (2.five cm) cubes 2 tablespoons plus 1 teaspoon (1.four ounces/40g) nice sea salt

½ teaspoon curing salt no. 1

2 tablespoons beaten dried Aleppo pepper

1 tablespoon finely chopped garlic

BRINED TONGUES

1 tablespoon peppercorns

1 tablespoon yellow mustard seeds three allspice berries

2 bay leaves

1 cup (270 g) nice sea salt

½ cup (one hundred g) sugar

four quarts (three.eight L) boiling water

6 lamb tongues or four red meat tongues

TONGUE POACHING LIQUID

eight cups (2 L) lamb or different meat broth (see Basic Rich Broth) 1 cup (240 ml) dry white wine

three cloves garlic,

smashed 1 big name anise, toasted

2 dried cayenne chiles

1 piece orange peel, approximately 2 with the aid of using 1 inch (five with the aid of using 2.five cm)

1 tablespoon nice sea salt

PANADE

¼ cup (60 ml) strained tongue poaching liquid

½ cup (one hundred twenty ml) heavy cream

¼ cup (15 g) clean bread crumbs

GARNISH

Reserved diced tongues

2 tablespoons coriander seeds, toasted and gently beaten

2 tablespoons finely chopped clean flat-leaf parsley
2 tablespoons finely chopped clean oregano I tablespoon
beaten dried Aleppo pepper
2 pounds (900 g) red meat again fats, sliced into skinny I-inch
(2.five cm) extensive strips, eight to ten inches (20 to twenty-
five cm) long, or I piece caul
fats, approximately eight with the aid of using 20 inches (20 with
the aid of using 50 cm)

Preheat the oven to 325°F (165°C). To make the forcemeat, unfold the peppercorns, cumin, and allspice on a baking sheet and toast for three to five minutes, till fragrant. Let cool completely, then switch to a spice grinder, upload the bay, and grind finely.

Place the lamb and fats in a big nonreactive bowl. To make the spice package, in a small bowl, integrate the freshly floor spices, sea salt, curing salt, Aleppo pepper, and garlic and blend properly. Mix the spice package with the meat, cover, and refrigerate overnight.

To make the brine for the tongues, vicinity the peppercorns, mustard seeds, allspice, and bay on a rectangular of cheesecloth, convey the corners together, and tie securely with wire to make a sachet (or use a muslin bag). Measure the salt and sugar right into a big box and toss withinside the sachet. Pour withinside the boiling water and stir to dissolve the salt and sugar. Let cool to room temperature, then upload the tongues and pinnacle with a plate or different weight to hold them submerged and refrigerate. If the usage of lamb tongues, go away them to brine for 12 hours. For red meat tongues, go away them to brine for twenty-four hours.

To make the poaching liquid, in a big saucepan, integrate the broth, wine, garlic, big name anise, chiles, orange peel, and salt and produce to a simmer over low heat. Cook for approximately half-hour to permit the flavors to meld.

Remove the tongues from the brine and discard the brine. Rinse the tongues in brief below bloodless going for walks water, then upload to the simmering poaching liquid. Cook till soft, approximately forty mins for lamb tongues and 1¼ hours for red meat tongues.

Using a slotted spoon, switch the tongues to a plate to cool. Strain the poaching liquid, booking sufficient for the panade. When the tongues have cooled, reduce them into ¼-inch (6 mm) cubes.

To make the panade, in a bowl, integrate the poaching liquid, cream, and crumbs and blend nicely.

Following the commands for grinding, suit the grinder with the smallest plate and grind the pro lamb and fats once. Fold withinside the panade and grind again. Add the cubed tongues, coriander, parsley, and oregano and blend nicely via way of means of hand for two to a few mins, till the farce pulls together. Cook a small pattern of the combination in a sauté pan, then kick back the pattern, flavor for seasonings, and alter if necessary.

Preheat the oven to 325°F (165°C). Bring a kettle full of water to a simmer. Sprinkle the Aleppo pepper calmly over the lower back fats (or caul fats, if the usage of), then line a terrine with the fats in order that the pepper- protected aspect is pressed in opposition to the terrine. Fill the terrine with the farce. Pack the farce nicely, tamping down after every addition after which tapping the terrine in opposition to the paintings floor to launch any air pockets. Fold the extra lower back fats over the pinnacle; trim any overlap and lid the terrine.

Fold a kitchen towel in 1/2 of and vicinity withinside the backside of a roasting pan big sufficient to house the terrine. Set the loaded terrine at the towel. Pour the simmering water into the roasting pan to attain one-1/3 of the manner up the edges of the terrine. Carefully vicinity withinside the oven and bake for approximately 1 hour, till a thermometer inserted into the middle of the terrine registers 140°F (60°C). Remove the roasting pan from the oven and lightly elevate the terrine out of the water tubtub. Let cool to room temperature, then refrigerate overnight.

To unmold the terrine, discover and vicinity the terrine in a hot-water tubtub for approximately 30 seconds to soften the fats lightly at the outside and unfasten the lowest and aspects from the mold. Remove from the water tubtub, invert onto a slicing board, and raise off the mold. Slice as a whole lot as you propose on serving, then wrap the the rest nicely and keep withinside the fridge for up to at least one week.

Duck Terrine with Brandied Prunes

DUCK TERRINE WITH BRANDIED PRUNES

At the Fatted Calf, we hold each sparkling and dried culmination in brandy. They make wonderful accompaniments to roasted and cured meats and are delectable gildings for savory terrines. Brandied prunes, laid down the middle of this duck terrine, are as visually dramatic as they may be delicious. Serve complete slices of this terrine with its fashionable prune garnish along a soft frisée salad or atop heat slices of brioche.

MAKES ONE 3-POUND (1.FOUR KG) TERRINE
   FORCEMEAT
1½ pounds (680 g) boneless, skinless duck meat, reduce into 1- inch (2.five cm) cubes

12 ounces (340 g) boneless red meat picnic, reduce into 1-inch

(2.five cm) cubes
eight ounces (225 g) red meat lower back fats, reduce into
1inch (2.five cm) cubes 1 teaspoon black peppercorns
½ teaspoon white peppercorns
2 allspice berries
1 complete clove
1 small dried bay leaf
1 tablespoon plus 1½ teaspoons best sea salt
¼ teaspoon floor ginger
½ teaspoon piment d'Espelette
¼ teaspoon curing salt no. 1
    PANADE
¼ cup (60 ml) duck broth (see Basic Rich Broth)
¼ cup (60 ml) brandied prunes liquor
½ cup (one hundred twenty ml) heavy cream
¼ cup (15 g) sparkling bread crumbs
    GARNISH
2 tablespoons chopped sparkling thyme
2 tablespoons chopped sparkling flat-leaf parsley
12 brandied prunes (see Dried Fruit in Brandy)
1 piece caul fats, approximately eight with the aid of using 20
inches (20 with the aid of using 50 cm), or 1 duck pores and
skin (see Four Ways to Line a Terrine)

To make the forcemeat, location the duck, red meat, and fats in a massive nonreactive bowl. To make the spice package, in a spice grinder, integrate the black and white peppercorns, allspice, clove, and bay and grind finely. Transfer to a small bowl, upload the salt, ginger, *piment d'Espelette*, and curing salt, and blend nicely. Mix the spice package with the beef, cover, and refrigerate in a single day.

To make the panade, in a small bowl, integrate the broth, liquor, cream, and bread crumbs and blend nicely.

Following the commands for grinding, match the grinder with the smallest plate and grind the beef once. Fold withinside the panade and grind again. Add the parsley and thyme and blend with the aid of using hand for two to a few minutes, till the farce pulls together. Cook a small pattern of the aggregate in a

sauté pan, then relax the pattern, flavor for seasonings, and modify if necessary.

Preheat the oven to 325°F (165°C). Bring a kettle full of water to a simmer. Line a terrine with the returned fats. Pack 1/2 of the farce into the lowest of the terrine. Lay the prunes in a line lengthwise down the middle, ensuring there aren't anyt any gaps among them. Pack the opposite 1/2 of of the farce on pinnacle of the prunes. The farce have to be stage with the lip of the terrine. Fold the extra caul fats or duck pores and skin over the pinnacle; trim any overlap and lid the terrine.

Fold a kitchen towel in 1/2 of and location withinside the backside of a roasting pan massive sufficient to deal with the terrine. Set the terrine at the towel. Pour the simmering water into the roasting pan to attain onethird of the manner up the perimeters of the terrine. Carefully location withinside the oven and bake for approximately 1 hour, till a thermometer inserted into the middle of the terrine registers 140°F (60°C). Remove the roasting pan from the oven and lightly carry the terrine out of the water tubtub. Let cool to room temperature, then refrigerate in a single day.

To unmold the terrine, discover and location the terrine in a hot-water tubtub for approximately 30 seconds to soften the fats lightly at the outside and unfasten the lowest and aspects from the mold. Remove from the water tubtub, invert onto a reducing board, and raise off the mold. Slice as lots as you intend on serving, then wrap the the rest nicely and shop withinside the fridge for up to at least one week.

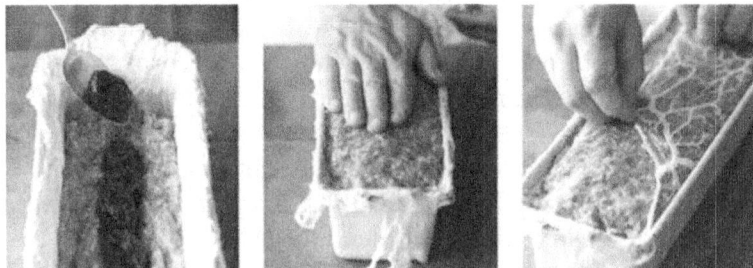

Galantines

Nothing harks returned to the coolest antique days of conventional French haute delicacies pretty like a galantine. A chicken is boned and full of a forcemeat embellished with slivers of sparkling black truffle or studded with nuts or fruit. The complete issue is rolled and tied, then poached and chilled in its cooking liquid, sliced and served bloodless along a bit salad or as a part of an assiette de charcuterie on the begin of a meal. Très classique!

The phrase galantine is concept to return back from the antique French phrase for Chicken, *geline; hence,* galantines are basically crafted from poultry. Chicken, guinea hen, duck, pheasant, and different recreation birds can all be used to make stylish and fantastic galantines. To begin, all the bones are cautiously eliminated with out making any tears withinside the pores and skin (see Whole Boned Bird). Next, a flavorful broth is crafted from the bones in an effort to be used to prepare dinner dinner the galantine later. For a few galantines, you may depart a few or all of the beef connected to the pores and skin; for others, the beef turns into a part of the stuffing, or forcemeat. Any meat separated from the pores and skin is normally mixed with red meat or different meats and marinated in a single day as you will for sausage or a terrine. The subsequent day, the beef is floor to provide a forcemeat. The livers and gizzards may be floor along side the beef or stored and used as a garnish. The forcemeat is crammed into the pores and skin, the complete bundle is formed right into a cylinder and tied or rolled in cheesecloth, after which the galantine is submerged in liquid and slowly poached till it reaches an inner temperature of approximately 145°F (63°C). Finally, the galantine is chilled in its poaching liquid to assist it to take in extra taste from the liquid and to preserve it wet and succulent.

To serve the galantine, it's miles eliminated from its poaching liquid. If you like, you could lessen the poaching liquid and use it to glaze the galantine. Slice the galantine into rounds and serve.

Veal and Chicken Galantine

VEAL AND CHICKEN GALANTINE

This galantine, studded with inexperienced olives and pro with sparkling herbs, makes an excellent first route or luncheon dish. Although its practise is labor-intensive, the galantine will hold for as much as four days withinside the fridge, so experience loose to prepare dinner dinner it earlier of serving.

MAKES ONE 3½-POUND (1.6 KG) GALANTINE
  FORCEMEAT

1 chook, four to five pounds (1.eight to
2.three kg) 12 ounces (340 g) beef
returned fat
eight ounces (225 g) lean veal meat from leg or shoulder
four ounces (a hundred and fifteen g) pancetta,
selfmade or save-sold 1 teaspoon yellow mustard
seeds, toasted
¾ teaspoon black peppercorns
¼ teaspoon white peppercorns
1 tablespoon plus 1½ teaspoons first-rate sea salt
¼ teaspoon curing salt no. 1
⅛ teaspoon floor mace
½ teaspoon floor cayenne
   POACHING LIQUID
Bones from the chook, plus 2 pounds (900 g)
extra chook bones and feet
½ cup (a hundred and
twenty ml) brandy 1
dried bay leaf
1 tablespoon first-rate sea salt
   PANADE
¼ cup (60 ml) dry white wine
¼ cup (60 ml) heavy cream
¼ cup (15 g) sparkling bread crumbs
   GARNISH
½ cup (70 g) pitted and sliced picholine or Castelvetrano olives
¼ cup (15 g) chopped sparkling flat-leaf
parsley 2 tablespoons chopped sparkling
thyme

Follow the commands for Whole Boned Bird. Once the beef is absolutely off the bone, trim any glands or blood vessels off of the beef. Carefully do away with the beef from the pores and skin, once more ensuring to keep away from puncturing holes withinside the pores and skin. Wrap the pores and skin in plastic wrap and refrigerate.

Weigh 1½ pounds (680 g) of the chook meat for the galantine and store any more for any other use. Cut the chook, fat, veal, and pancetta into 1-inch (2.five cm) cubes and vicinity in a huge nonreactive bowl.

To make the spice package, in a spice grinder, integrate the mustard seeds and the black and white peppercorns and grind finely. Transfer to a small bowl, upload the ocean salt, curing salt, mace, and cayenne, and blend nicely. Mix the spice package with the meats, cowl, and refrigerate overnight. To make the poaching liquid, chop the bones and make a easy bone broth (see Basic Rich Broth). Strain the broth and refrigerate overnight, uncovered. The following day, do away with any solidified fat from the pinnacle of the broth, then carry the broth to a simmer in a narrow, tall pot. Measure the liquid and decrease if vital to yield three quarts (2.eight L). Add the brandy, bay, and salt and flavor for seasonings. It must be very flavorful and nicely pro. Set liquid apart till you're prepared to poach the galantine.

To make the panade, in a small bowl, integrate the wine, cream, and crumbs and blend nicely. Assemble the garnish ingredients.

Following the commands for grinding, match the grinder with the smallest plate and grind the meats once. Fold withinside the panade and the garnish and blend via way of means of hand for two to a few minutes, till the farce holds collectively and the garnish is calmly distributed. Cook a small pattern of the combination in a sauté pan, then sit back the pattern, flavor for seasonings, and regulate if vital.

Spread the pores and skin out on a slicing board, with the longest aspect closest to you. Lay the farce lengthwise down the center and mould right into a cylinder. Fold the longest fringe of the pores and skin over the farce and roll the cylinder farfar from you to cowl absolutely. Pat and press the cylinder to launch any air wallet and create a noticeably uniform shape. Tuck the open ends well underneath. Wrap snugly in numerous layers of cheesecloth and stable every stop tightly with butcher's twine.

Return the pot preserving the poaching liquid to the range pinnacle and warmth to 160°F (70°C). Carefully slip the galantine into the liquid and poach lightly over very low heat, turning the galantine from time to time and spooning the liquid over it to make sure even cooking, for approximately 1¼ hours till a thermometer inserted into the middle registers 145°F (63°C).

Remove the pot from the range and permit the galantine to chill at room temperature in its poaching liquid for approximately 30 minutes. Place a plate on pinnacle of the galantine to hold it submerged withinside the liquid withinside the pot, then refrigerate the pot overnight.

The following day, do away with the galantine from the pot and unwrap from the cheesecloth. Slice into rounds ½ inch (12 mm) thick to serve. Slice as a good deal as you propose on serving, then wrap the the rest nicely and save withinside the fridge for as much as four days.

COU FARCI

This dish is a vacation uniqueness withinside the Gascony location of France and on the Fatted Calf. *Cou is the French phrase for "neck" and farci means "filled."* In this recipe, the forcemeat of red meat and veal is studded with braised chestnuts and chunks of cured foie gras, filled into goose or duck necks, and poached in a pro broth.

MAKES FOUR STUFFED DUCK NECKS OR 2 STUFFED GOOSE NECKS; SERVES EIGHT AS A STARTER
   FORCEMEAT
1 ¼ pounds (570 g) boneless veal shoulder, reduce into 1-inch (2.five cm) cubes
12 ounces (340g) boneless red meat picnic, reduce into 1-inch (2.five cm) cubes
eight ounces (225 g) red meat again fats, reduce into 1inch (2.five cm) cubes 1 teaspoon coriander seeds, toasted
1 teaspoon white peppercorns
¾ teaspoon yellow mustard seeds
1 entire clove
⅛ teaspoon floor mace
⅛ teaspoon freshly grated
nutmeg 1 allspice berry
¾ teaspoon dried thyme
1 tablespoon exceptional
sea salt
   GARNISH
1 cup peeled chestnuts, sparkling or frozen

2 cups (480 ml) duck broth (see **Basic Rich Broth**)

¼ cup (60 ml) brandy

I teaspoon exceptional

sea salt

2 ounces (fifty five g) **Foie Gras Torchon with Port and Quatre Épices**, finely diced

PANADE

¾ cup (a hundred and eighty

ml) heavy cream I

tablespoon brandy

¼ cup (15 g) sparkling bread

crumbs four duck necks, or 2

goose necks

POACHING LIQUID

eight cups (2 L) duck or hen broth (see **Basic Rich Broth**)

¼ cup (60 ml) brandy

I ½ teaspoons exceptional sea salt

Place the veal, red meat, and fats in a nonreactive bowl. To make the spice package, in a spice grinder, integrate the coriander, peppercorns, mustard seeds, clove, allspice, and thyme and grind finely. Transfer to a bowl, upload the salt, and blend well. Mix the spice package with the meat, cover, and refrigerate overnight.

To gather the garnish, in a saucepan, integrate the chestnuts, broth, and brandy, deliver to a simmer over low warmth, and prepare dinner dinner for approximately 20 minutes, till the chestnuts are tender. Remove from the warmth, season with salt, and refrigerate to relax.

Using a slotted spoon, switch the chilled chestnuts to a reducing board, booking the liquid, then region the chestnuts. Set apart with the liquid and foie gras.

To make the panade, in a small bowl, integrate the cream, brandy, and crumbs and blend well. Set apart.

Following the commands for grinding, match the grinder with the smallest plate and grind the meats once. Fold withinside the panade and grind again. Fold withinside the chestnuts and their cooking liquid and the foie gras and blend with the aid of using hand for approximately 1 to two minutes, till the farce holds collectively and the garnishes are calmly distributed. Cook a small pattern of the aggregate in a sauté pan, then relax the pattern, flavor for seasonings, and alter if necessary.

Prepare the necks for stuffing. With the top of a pointy knife, make a circle across the base of a neck, simply above the wishbone, urgent all of the manner to the bone. Gently pull the pores and skin absolutely farfar from the

bone, turning the pores and skin interior out. Trim away any blood vessels or glands. Using a trussing needle and butcher's wire, sew closed the widest cease of neck. Knot the wire at each ends. Repeat with the final neck(s).

To make the poaching liquid, in a big saucepan, integrate the broth, brandy, and salt, vicinity at the range pinnacle, and warmth to 160°F (70°C). While the liquid is heating, gather a sausage stuffer and stuff the necks from the open cease as you'll salami (Casing, Linking, Looping, and Tying). Tie the open ends tightly closed with butcher's wire.

Transfer the filled necks to the poaching liquid and poach lightly over very low warmth for approximately 25 to half-hour or till a thermometer inserted into the middle of a neck registers 140°F (60°C).

Remove the pot from the range and permit the necks to chill at room temperature of their poaching liquid for approximately half-hour. Place a plate on pinnacle of the necks to maintain them submerged withinside the liquid withinside the pot, then refrigerate the pot overnight.

The following day, dispose of the necks from the pot and slice into rounds 1 inch (2.five cm) thick to serve. Unsliced leftovers will maintain withinside the fridge for four to five days.

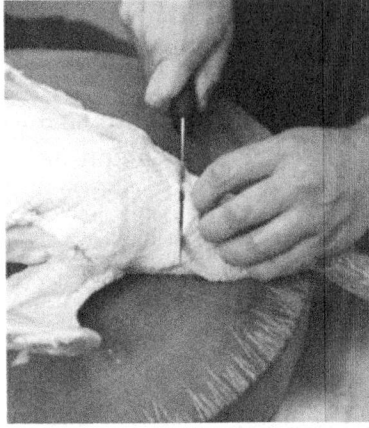

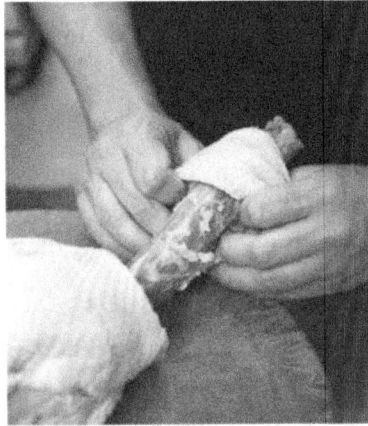

Liver and Foie Gras Preparations

All Foie gras is liver however now no longer all liver is foie gras. Foie gras, literally "fats liver" in French, is the end result of gavage, a technique of fattening a duck or goose with a purpose to produce a totally big, fatty liver with a meaty, silky texture and delicate, nutty flavor.

Raw foie gras is normally bought whole. Each liver includes a huge and a small lobe. The livers are graded A via C for best. We tremendously suggest which you buy simplest grade A foie gras, that's of advanced best, an awful lot simpler to put together, and simplest barely greater steeply-priced than grade B. Grade C foie gras is of bad best and normally simplest utilized in industrial preparations. Good foie gras could have an attractive shadeation that degrees from cream to light peach, with very little discoloration or blemishing.

LOVE THE LIVER OR LEAVE IT: THE FOIEGRAS CONTROVERSY

In recent years, gavage, the process of feeding ducks and geese by hand for fattening their liver, has been at the center of the foie gras controversy. It is important to decide for yourself whether or not you are comfortable with specific aspects of animal husbandry and to learn all of the facts before coming to a conclusion.

For most of their lives, ducks and geese that are destined to produce foie gras live on a farm just like their regular counterparts. In the last 2 to 3 weeks of their lives, they are fed by the method known as gavage two or three times each day. A small tube is inserted into bird's throat and the bird is fed a mixture that usually contains some cooked corn. This practice prompts two questions: is it force-feeding and is it cruel? To answer these questions, you must keep a couple of things in mind. Ducks and geese are waterfowl and their throats, unlike ours, are designed to swallow whole, live, wriggling creatures. A food sac at the base of their throat allows them to store many meals' worth of food as they hunt. Their windpipe is located at the center of their tongue, which eliminates any gag reflex during feeding. Gorging before migration is a natural part of waterfowl life, and they are adapted to store great quantities of fat in their livers without harming themselves. The fattened liver is healthy and normal, and if the birds were to return to regular feedings, their liver would return to its prefattened size.

Cases of animal cruelty have resulted from the manufacturing of foie gras, simply as many instances of animal cruelty have befell with all different styles of farming. The ducks and geese are a treasured commodity and vital to the farmer's livelihood. Stress or mistreatment will bring about inferior foie gras and a loss for farmers. Responsible farmers care deeply approximately their fees and take the time to provide them an amazing life.

Foie gras is a treat, now no longer some thing you devour everyday. If you need to indulge now and again, get the great things from a best source.

The ordinary, unfattened livers of duck, goose, fowl and different rooster also are splendidly flavored and may be used to provide an array of charcuterie. Good-best rooster produces good-best livers, so constantly purchase your livers from a farm you trust. Livers want to be flawlessly sparkling. Look for livers which can be whole, with a deep pink wine shadeation and no discernable odor.

Preparing Liver

Both ordinary livers and foie gras should be wiped clean and trimmed earlier than the use of. To put together sparkling duck or different rooster livers for cooking, rinse in short in a colander beneathneath a mild movement of bloodless jogging water. Pat dry with a paper towel and vicinity on a reducing board. Use one hand to keep the liver in vicinity and the opposite to tug any filaments of connective tissue or veins from it. Then, the use of a paring knife, trim away any discolored regions or bile spots. Refrigerate the livers till prepared to use.

To put together foie gras for cooking, eliminate the liver from the fridge and permit to mood at room temperature for approximately 1 hour. Foie gras is simplest to paintings with whilst it's miles simply barely cooler than room temperature. Using a paring knife, break up the foie gras alongside the seam to split the huge and small lobes. Turn the lobes reduce aspect up for your reducing board. Using the top of the knife, disclose the huge vein that runs from the pinnacle to bottom, then slip the knife beneathneath the top of the vein and lightly tug it out, preferably in a single piece. Needle-nostril pliers may be reachable for this sensitive operation. Using the identical method, pull out some other seen blood vessels. Foie gras within reason forgiving, and any usable foie gras displaced at some point of cleansing may be lightly prodded lower back into vicinity.

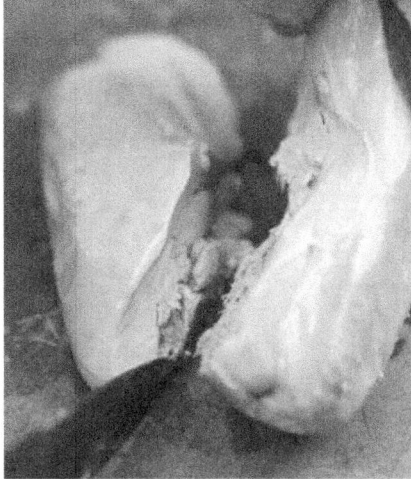

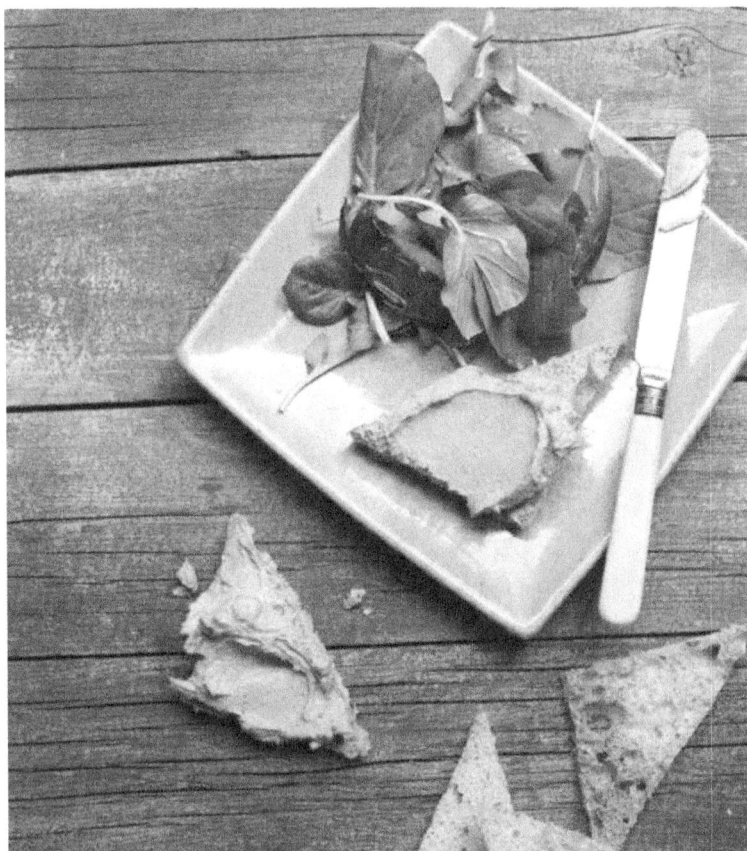

Duck Liver Mousse with Armagnac Cream

DUCK LIVER MOUSSE WITH ARMAGNAC CREAM

"Sex on toast" became how one Fatted Calf ordinary defined wedges of toasted pan de mie crowned with this decadent duck liver mousse. In this suited preparation, sautéed duck livers are enriched with butter after which exalted with Armagnac whipped cream to create a silky, luxurious unfold to be loved with toast points, in a Vietnamese-fashion banh mi, or,

with the blinds drawn, au naturel—immediately from the

crock with a spoon.

MAKES ONE 6-CUP (I.FOUR L) TERRINE
2½ pounds (1.2 kg) organized duck livers, wiped clean and
trimmed I tablespoon high-quality sea salt, plus a pinch
½ teaspoon freshly floor pepper
¼ teaspoon freshly floor white pepper
½ teaspoon curing salt no. I (optional)
2 tablespoons rendered duck fats
½ cup (one hundred twenty ml) duck gelée, or 2 cups (480 ml)
duck broth (see Basic Rich Broth) decreased to ½ cup (one
hundred twenty ml) then seasoned
with I teaspoon high-quality sea salt
½ cup (one hundred twenty ml) Armagnac
I½ cups (340 g) unsalted butter, at room temperature
I cup (240 ml) heavy cream

Place the livers in a nonreactive bowl. Season with the 1 tablespoon salt, the black and white pepper, and the curing salt, then cowl and refrigerate overnight.

In a heavy sauté pan, soften the duck fats over medium-excessive heat. When the fats starts to sizzle, upload the livers and sauté for approximately five minutes. They have to be rosy at the internal and yielding to touch however now no longer squishy. Turn out onto a platter to cool. Refrigerate, uncovered, for two hours.

Divide the cooked livers into three equal batches. Put one-third of the livers into a food processor and puree for 3 minutes. Slowly add one-third of the gelée and 1 tablespoon of Armagnac, followed by onethird of the butter. Process for another 2 to 3 minutes, until the mixture is very smooth. Using a rubber spatula, scrape the puree into a bowl. Repeat with the remaining two batches of livers, adding onethird of the gelée, 1 tablespoon of Armagnac, and one-third of the butter to each batch.

Stir the 3 batches together, then flavor for seasoning and regulate if necessary. Set a fine-mesh sieve or tamis over a bowl, then byskip the

puree thru it with the aid of using scraping small quantities over the mesh floor with a spatula or plastic bench scraper.

In a bowl, the usage of a whisk, whip the cream to gentle peaks. Whisk the closing Armagnac and a pinch of salt into the cream, then fold the cream into the liver puree and flavor for seasoning.

If you'll be serving the mousse en terrine, percent it into an earthenware crock. Alternatively, line a 6-cup (1.four L) terrine with plastic wrap, permitting it to overhang the edges with the aid of using at the least three inches (7.five cm), and fill with the mousse. Bring up the overhang to cowl the top, then refrigerate for at the least three hours to set. To flip out the mousse, take away it from the fridge and invert it onto a slicing board, then cautiously elevate off the terrine. Carefully peel away the plastic wrap and slice to serve. The mousse will hold withinside the fridge for as much as four days.

Foie Gras Terrine with Madeira Gelée

FOIE GRAS TERRINE WITH MADEIRA GELÉE

In this easy however lovely preparation, an entire lobe of foie gras is pro with fleur de sel, nestled right into a terrine, and cooked till simply set, then protected with a layer of Madeira gelée. The impact is a pride to each the attention and the palate. The glossy, caramel-coloured gelée surrounds the baked foie gras, seeping into the cracks on its floor and accentuating the opulent,

nutty taste of the liver. Sauternes or vin santo makes an first-rate opportunity to the Madeira.

SERVES 8
1 complete grade A foie gras
Fleur de sel
1 cup (240 ml) duck gelée or exceedingly pro gelatinous duck broth (see Basic Broth Making, step 12)
1 cup (240 ml) Madeira
Hot brioche slices, for serving

Clean and trim the foie gras as directed in Preparing Liver. Lightly season the liver on all facets with the fleur de sel. Place in a nonreactive dish or container, cowl, and refrigerate in a single day.

In a saucepan, integrate the gelée and Madeira, region over medium heat, and simmer for approximately 15 minutes, till decreased with the aid of using 1/2 of. Set apart to chill.

Preheat the oven to 275°F (135°C). Remove the foie gras from the fridge and allow mood at room temperature for approximately 30 minutes.

Bring a kettle filled with water to a simmer. Press the smaller lobe on the bottom of a small earthenware terrine or 1-quart (960 ml) soufflé dish, then mold the larger lobe around it. Fold a kitchen towel in half and place in the bottom of a roasting pan large enough to accommodate the terrine. Set the loaded terrine on the towel. Pour the simmering water into the roasting pan to reach one-third of the way up the sides of the terrine. Carefully place into the oven and bake for 20 to 25 minutes, until a thermometer inserted into the center of the foie gras registers 120°F (49°C). Remove from the oven and gently lift the terrine from the water bath.

Ladle off as a good deal fats as feasible with out detrimental the form of the liver. Reserve the fats for any other use. Allow the terrine to chill for 1 hour, then pour the decreased Madeira and gelée over the top.
Refrigerate in a single day to permit the flavors to marry.

To serve, allow the terrine come to room temperature, then reduce slices immediately out of the dish and unfold onto warm brioche. Serve with plenty

of Champagne. Tightly wrap any leftover terrine in plastic wrap and keep withinside the fridge for as much as five days.

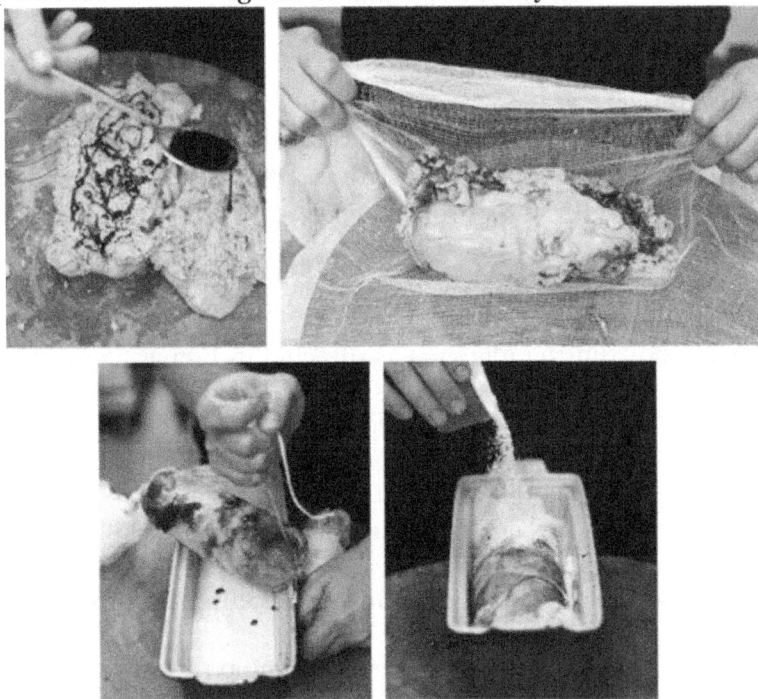

Foie Gras Torchon with Port and Quatre Épices

FOIE GRAS TORCHON WITH

PORT AND QUATRE ÉPICES

Torchon is the French phrase for a "rag" or "dish towel," and a foie gras au torchon is a foie gras this is pro after which wrapped in a towel or cheesecloth to mildew it previous to cooking. Some torchons are poached, however this torchon is buried in salt to "prepare dinner dinner." The end result is a dense, firm, buttery, well-pro foie gras with a fetching, darkish inlay of decreased port and quatre épices. Slice the torchon and serve with heat brioche, shave with a vegetable peeler over a easy arugula salad, or pinnacle a steak warm off the grill with a thick coin of its buttery goodness.

SERVES 6 TO 8

I complete grade A foie gras
Fleur de sel or Maldon sea salt
2 cups (480 ml) port
I ½ teaspoons quatre épices
five pounds (2.three kg) high-
quality sea salt

Clean and put together the foie gras in keeping with the commands in Preparing Liver. Lightly season the liver on all aspects with fleur de sel. Place in a nonreactive dish or box, cowl, and refrigerate overnight.

In a saucepan, slowly prepare dinner dinner the port over low warmness for 20 to 30 minutes, till decreased to approximately ¼ cup (60 ml). Pour right into a small box, cowl, and refrigerate overnight.

The following day, lay the foie gras on a reducing board or platter. Drizzle the decreased port over the reduce facet of every lobe, accompanied through a dusting of the quatre épices. Allow to marinate at room temperature for 1 hour.

Cut a double layer of cheesecloth approximately two times the period of the foie gras. Lay the massive lobe lengthwise, reduce facet up, at the cheesecloth. Place the smaller lobe, reduce facet down, on pinnacle of the bigger lobe. Fold the brink of the cheesecloth closest to you over the foie gras and squeeze to shape a cylinder kind of 2 inches (five cm) in diameter. Foie gras is commonly fats and really malleable, so don't worry approximately unfavourable the liver. Roll the foie tightly withinside the cheesecloth and steady the open ends with wire. You need to have a neat little parcel of rather uniform dimensions that appears now no longer not like a salami.

Pour kind of one-1/3 of the high-quality sea salt into the lowest of a deep box massive sufficient to deal with the torchon comfortably. Nestle the torchon on pinnacle of the salt, then cowl absolutely with the last high-quality sea salt. The torchon need to be buried with out a part of it seen above the pinnacle layer of salt. Cover and refrigerate for three days. Gently unearth the torchon from the salt, dismiss any salt that adheres to the cheesecloth, snip the wire that secured the ends closed, and punctiliously unroll the foie gras. Cut a slice off the give up to taste. It need to be exceedingly pro, rich, and really firm. If it appears a bit bland,

roll up the torchon in a clean piece of doubled cheesecloth and bury it withinside the identical salt for 12 to 24 hours longer.

Serve the torchon as cautioned withinside the headnote. Tightly wrap any unused component in plastic wrap and shop withinside the fridge for up to one week.

Braised Ham Hocks

FOUR

BRINED, CURED & SMOKED

Necessity is probably what drove us to find

out the magic of dry curing, smoking, and brining in our quest for keeping

meat for survival. But possibly it's miles our human nature, our choice to govern the elements, that led us to tinker with fire, water, air, and salty earth, turning necessity into the exceedingly cultivated crafts of brining, dry curing, and smoking. These 3 finely tuned techniques of upkeep are frequently intertwined to create the salty, smoky, candy, and spiced meats that historically tide us over in the course of our lean instances and accompany us on our journeys, offering sustenance and some thing extra: taste that we lengthy for. Even today, while refrigeration, current canning techniques, and different technology have rendered those historical upkeep techniques obsolete, we starvation for bacon, have a hankering for an awesome pastrami sandwich, and can not byskip up a chunk of salty candy ham.

Brined

Think of a brine as a scrumptious tubtub that seasons, tenderizes, and enables to each keep meat and hold it juicy in the course of cooking. It may be as easy as water combined with salt or extra complex, containing a bunch of fragrant ingredients. How lengthy you brine and what is going into the brine relies upon on the kind and length of the beef reduce and the preferred outcome. The meat is very well submerged on this tubtub for everywhere from some hours to gain easy seasoning for smaller cuts, to 3 days for large cuts, or for as much as numerous weeks while upkeep is the goal.

Brining for Flavor

When you need to season meat very well and keep moisture all through roasting or smoking, brining is the manner to go. It is mainly useful for more difficult or lean cuts, big cuts, or cuts at the bone. Through osmosis, brines penetrate the beef extra efficaciously than normal salting, in order that the indoors of the beef is simply as flavorful because the floor. Brined meats generally tend to prepare dinner dinner at a barely quicker rate, and brining can offset the moisture loss that generally takes place all through roasting, grilling, and smoking, preserving the beef moist. And in case you manifest to prepare dinner dinner your brined roast a touch extra than you supposed to, brining gives a cushion for variance, preserving your meat juicy and delicious.

Meats to Brine
Almost any meat may be brined, however beef and rooster are the maximum typically brined meats. Both of them want to be cooked to a better inner temperature than different roasting or grilling beef, lamb, or goat cuts, and brining offers the beef delivered moisture to assist it keep juiciness, even if cooked to better temperatures. Very lean cuts, which include beef loin or hen breast, or meats so one can be smoked or sluggish roasted for a protracted time, which include spareribs, gain from brining for a great deal the equal reason. Unevenly fashioned cuts, cuts made from numerous muscles, big cuts, or very bony cuts, which include an entire ham or a turkey, additionally take advantage of the cappotential of a brine to disperse seasonings very well and evenly. Brining may even tenderize more difficult cuts, which include leg or shoulder muscles.

Saltwater Science
There are essential approaches that arise whilst meat is brined: osmosis and protein modification. Osmosis takes place whilst there may be an choppy stability of solvent molecules on both facet of a membrane: solvent redistriButes itself and restores equilibrium via way of means of travelling from the vicinity of better awareness to the vicinity of decrease awareness. When meat is located in a salty brine, osmosis is mechanically triggered. Because the brine surrounding the beef has a better awareness of salt than the liquid in the muscle, the muscle attracts withinside the brine, permitting the seasonings to permeate the beef. But

the salt that interacts with the proteins adjustments them. Cells plump and water that might usually go with the drift out to create equilibrium turns into trapped. The cells each attract and maintain extra water. The salt additionally acts on a number of the proteins, breaking down their structure, loosening the relationship among cells, and inflicting historically hard cuts of meat to turn out to be extra tender.

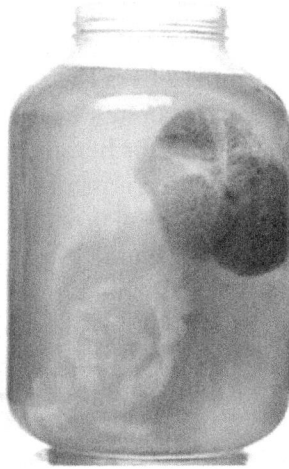

Brine Ingredients

The key to a brine is salt, and what sort of salt you operate relies upon at the period of time the beef may be submerged withinside the brine. Fine sea salt is usually recommended because it dissolves without difficulty in water. Always weigh the salt for a brine to make sure accuracy.

Sugar is used for flavoring and facilitates to stability the salt. It additionally gives a bonus: any sugar at the floor of the beef will caramelize all through cooking, giving the beef a adorable golden sheen.

Aromatics, which include spices, herbs, garlic, and onions, may be delivered to a brine to impart a lot of diffused flavors to meat. Be certain to feature aromatics to the brine whilst it's miles nonetheless heat, in order that the flavors will infuse very well into the liquid.

Brining Basics

1. Gather your gadget and ensure you've got got adequate area for refrigeration or have a completely big cooler and masses of ice. Choose a field this is made from tough food-grade plastic and approximately two times as big because the reduce of meat you may be brining. You may additionally want a heavy plate or different weight to maintain the beef submerged withinside the brine.

2. Make the brine an afternoon in advance or in advance withinside the day in order that it has masses of time to chill to room temperature.

3. Use particularly warm or boiling water to dissolve the salt and sugar very well withinside the brine.

4. Add the aromatics whilst the brine continues to be warm to facilitate the discharge of flavor. The aromatics may be tied in a cheesecloth sachet in case you do now no longer need to should choose them off of the beef after brining.

5. Allow the brine to chill to room temperature or simply beneath earlier than putting the beef withinside the brine. Never area meat right into a warm or maybe heat brine.

6. Fully submerge the beef. Make certain that every one of the beef is beneath the floor of the brine. Top with a heavy plate, if necessary, to make sure it stays submerged.

7. Refrigerate the beef withinside the brine at once and maintain it cold (at the least 40°F/ 4°C).

8. Label the brine field with the contents, date, and time, so you will consider to tug the beef from the brine at precisely the proper time. This is specifically useful in case you are brining for numerous days or brining numerous cuts at once.

9. Allow brined meat to air-dry. Once you put off the beef from the brine, region it on a tray or platter covered with a kitchen towel and permit to air-dry withinside the refrigerator. The floor need to be absolutely dry earlier than cooking, in order that the beef

will brown properly.

10. Discard used brine. Never reuse a brine.

ALL-PURPOSE POULTRY BRINE

This easy brine is right for seasoning the whole lot from small recreation hens to huge turkeys. Poultry is an specifically true candidate for brining. The breasts and legs of maximum birds prepare dinner dinner at distinct rates. Brining allows the leaner breast meat live wet and juicy even as the legs end cooking. Be positive to permit the chook to dry absolutely earlier than cooking to make sure crispy skin. The chart underneath lists the quantity of brine essential for birds of diverse sizes and the brining time for each. Depending on the dimensions of your chook, you could want to divide or multiply this recipe to yield the desired quantity of brine.

MAKES ABOUT FOUR QUARTS(THREE.EIGHT L)
7 ounces (2 hundred grams) pleasant sea salt
three.7 ounces (a hundred and five grams) sugar four quarts (three.eight L) boiling water

Place the salt and sugar in a big nonreactive field. Pour withinside the water and stir to dissolve the salt and sugar. Cover loosely and permit cool for as a minimum four hours or for as much as overnight, till cooled to room temperature.

Lightly rinse the rooster to be brined and pat dry. Submerge the rooster withinside the brine, pinnacle it with a plate to maintain it submerged, and refrigerate for the favored brining time.

Line a tray or platter with a kitchen towel. Remove the rooster from the brine and discard the brine. Place the rooster at the organized tray and refrigerate exposed till the floor is very well dry.

Small birds
Weight: I to two pounds (450 to 900 g)
Brine time: 6 to twelve hours
Brine amount: 2 to three quarts (960 ml to two.eight L)

Medium birds
Weight: 2 to five pounds (900 g to two.three kg)
Brine time: 12 to 24 hours
Brine amount: four quarts (three.eight L)

Large birds
Weight: five to ten pounds (2.three to four.five kg)
Brine time: 24 to 36 hours
Brine amount: 6 to eight quarts (five.7 to 7.four L)

Extra-big birds
Weight: 10 to twenty pounds (four.five to nine kg)
Brine time: 36 to forty eight hours
Brine amount: eight to sixteen quarts (7.four to fifteen L)

GARLIC BRINE

This all-cause red meat brine may be used to season and tenderize shoulder, loin, sparerib, and different cuts. Make the brine the day earlier than to permit the flavors of the garlic and spices to permeate the brine. The chart underneath lists the quantity of brine essential for cuts of diverse sizes and the brining time for each. Depending on the dimensions of your cut, you could want to divide or multiply this recipe to yield the desired quantity of brine.

MAKES FOUR QUARTS (THREE.EIGHT L)
20 cloves garlic, gently
overwhelmed 2 tablespoons
peppercorns
2 tablespoons yellow mustard seeds
2 teaspoons chile flakes
2 teaspoons allspice berries
eight entire cloves
four dried bay leaves
eight ounces (225 g) pleasant sea salt
nine.6 ounces (270 g) sugar
four quarts (three.eight liters) boiling water

Place the garlic, peppercorns, mustard seeds, chile flakes, allspice, cloves, and bay on a rectangular of cheesecloth, carry the corners together, and tie securely with wire to make a sachet (or use a muslin bag). Place the salt and sugar in a big nonreactive field. Pour withinside the boiling water and stir to dissolve the salt and sugar. Add the sachet, cowl the field loosely, and permit cool for as a minimum four hours or for as much as overnight, till cooled to room temperature.

Lightly rinse the beef to be brined and pat dry. Submerge the beef withinside the brine, pinnacle it with a plate or different weight to maintain it submerged, and refrigerate for the favored brining time.

Line a tray or platter with a kitchen towel. Remove the beef from the brine and discard the brine. Place the beef at the organized tray and refrigerate exposed till the floor is very well dry.

Loin or porterhouse chops Brine
time: eight to twelve hours
Brine amount 2 to three quarts (960 ml to two.eight L)

Spareribs, toddler lower back ribs, or
stomach Brine time: 12 to 24 hours
Brine amount four quarts (three.eight L)

Whole loin, shoulder, or leg roast Brine
time: forty eight to seventy two hours
Brine amount 6 to eight quarts (five.7 to 7.five L)

CIDER-BRINED PORK PORTERHOUSE CHOPS

Pork porterhouse chops, which comprise a move phase of each the loin and tenderloin, may be a elaborate to prepare dinner dinner flawlessly due to the fact the 2 muscle mass prepare dinner dinner at barely unique rates. Brining this reduce in bubbling tough apple cider guarantees that each facets of the chop live succulent and tender. This recipe requires searing after which cooking the chops withinside the oven; however, they're additionally splendid grilled or smoked. If porterhouse chops are unavailable, beef rib chops (see The Loin, Step 4a) are a excellent alternative.

SERVES 6
1 tablespoon black peppercorns
1 tablespoon yellow mustard seeds
three complete cloves
five allspice
berries three
dried bay leaves
nine ounces (255 g)
excellent sea salt eight
ounces (225 g) sugar
five quarts (four.7 L) boiling water
¾ cup (one hundred eighty ml) good-first-
rate tough apple cider 6 bone-in beef
porterhouse chops
1 tablespoon lard

Place the peppercorns, mustard seeds, cloves, allspice, and bay on a rectangular of cheesecloth, convey the corners together, and tie securely with wire to make a sachet (or use a muslin bag). Place the salt and sugar in a huge nonreactive box. Pour withinside the boiling water and stir to dissolve the salt and sugar. Add the sachet, cowl the box loosely, and allow cool for at the least four hours or for as much as overnight, till cooled to room temperature.

When the brine has cooled to room temperature, stir withinside the cider. Lightly rinse the chops and pat dry. Submerge the chops withinside the brine, pinnacle them with a plate or different weight to maintain them submerged, and refrigerate for forty eight hours.

Line a tray or platter with a kitchen towel. Remove the chops from the brine and discard the brine. Place the chops at the organized tray and refrigerate exposed till the floor is very well dry. (Once the chops are dry, they may be wrapped in plastic and saved for five days withinside the fridge or 6 weeks withinside the freezer.)

To prepare dinner dinner the chops, preheat the oven to 350°F (one hundred eighty°C). Remove the chops from the fridge and mood at room temperature for 20 to 30 mins.

Heat a huge, heavy ovenproof skillet over medium warmth. Add the lard and tilt the pan to coat the lowest evenly. Place the chops withinside the pan in an even, uncrowded layer. Brown them on one facet for approximately 7 mins. Turn the chops over, then slide the pan into the recent oven and prepare dinner dinner for approximately 10 mins greater, till golden brown. Serve warm.

Brining for Preservation

Brining meats is an age-vintage procedure of meals preservation. Simple salt brines will inhibit the increase of bacteria, however they're now no longer enough for lengthy storage. When you need to apply brining for keeping further to flavoring, you should upload curing salt, or salt mixed with sodium nitrate, to the brine (see bankruptcy 1 for greater on curing salts). Sodium nitrate kills the Clostridium botulinum spores than can reason lethal botulism at the side of different probably dangerous pathogens. Curing salt additionally offers brine-cured meats their function red color. Without the addition of nitrates, those meats could flip a completely unappealing colour of gray.

Brines with curing salt are made in addition to different brines besides that the curing salt should be stirred into the brine after it has cooled to room temperature. It can not be brought to warm or heat brine due to the fact warmth lessens its effectiveness. As an brought degree of success, a brine pump may be employed. Basic brine pumps, which can be to be had at

distinctiveness kitchen and butchery deliver stores and seem like large syringes, are used to inject the brine into thicker cuts or cuts at the bone to make sure it penetrates throughout. Injection additionally shortens the general brining time. Injecting brine isn't always an alternative choice to submerging the beef withinside the brine, however. Instead, it need to be executed at the side of submersion.

SMOKED HAM HOCKS

In the cooler months, smoked ham hocks are a staple

withinside the Fatted Calf kitchen. They make a flavorful addition to soups, beans, braised greens, or the Alsatian classic, Choucroute Garni. Foreshanks, which can be hocks reduce from the the front legs, are usually favored for this treatment, as they've a piece greater meat, however hind shanks may be brined and smoked as well.

MAKES FOUR SMOKED HOCKS
1 tablespoon black peppercorns
1 tablespoon yellow mustard seeds
five complete cloves
eight allspice
berries four dried
bay leaves
10 ounces (280 grams) sugar
eight ounces (225 grams)
excellent sea salt four quarts
(three.eight liters) boiling water
1 tablespoon curing salt no. 1
four skin-on, bone-in beef shanks, approximately 12 ounces (340 g) each

To make the brine, region the peppercorns, mustard seeds, cloves, allspice, and bay on a rectangular of cheesecloth, deliver the corners together, and tie securely with wire to make a sachet (or use a muslin bag). Place the sugar and salt in a massive nonreactive box. Pour withinside the boiling water and stir to dissolve the sugar and salt. Add the sachet, cowl the box loosely, and permit cool for at the least four hours or for as much as in a single day, till cooled to room temperature.

Stir the curing salt into the cooled brine. Lightly rinse the beef shanks. Using a brine pump, inject approximately ¼ cup (60 ml) of the brine into every shank subsequent to the bone. Submerge the shanks withinside the ultimate brine, pinnacle with a plate or different weight to maintain them submerged, and refrigerate for 10 days.

Line a tray or platter with a kitchen towel. Remove the shanks from the brine and discard the brine. Place the shanks at the organized tray and refrigerate exposed in a single day to dry thoroughly.

The following day, put together your smokehouse following the suggestions indexed for Hot and Cold Smoking. When the smoker reaches a temperature of 180°F (82°C), prepare dinner dinner the shanks for approximately three hours, till a thermometer inserted into the thickest a part of the beef now no longer touching bone registers 145°F (63°C).

Remove the hocks from the smoker and allow them to cool to room temperature. Wrap tightly in plastic wrap and refrigerate for up to two weeks or freeze for up to a few months.

BRAISED HAM HOCKS

To unharness the powerful taste and smooth, succulent texture of brined and smoked ham hocks, they ought to first be braised. We discover that maximum recipes that name for ham hocks fail to deal with them to a prolonged simmer that releases their complete potential. Many bean and soup recipes prepare dinner dinner greater unexpectedly than the hock, and despite the fact that the hock will make contributions taste and a touch fats to the pot, its meat will stay tough. The answer is to first braise the ham hock to smooth perfection, if you want to yield each precious braising liquor that may be used to enhance a pot of beans, braised greens, or soup and hock meat smooth sufficient to be served as is or shredded off the bone. See photo.

MAKES 2 BRAISED HOCKS
2 smoked ham hocks
eight cups (2 L) water or beef, chicken, or duck broth (see
Basic Rich Broth)
I dried bay leaf
I small yellow onion, halved

In a pot, integrate the hocks, water, bay, and onion and region over medium heat. Bring to a simmer, flip down the warmth to low, and prepare dinner dinner slowly simply underneath a simmer. Cover or partly cowl the pot if the liquid appears to be evaporating. Cook the hocks for approximately three hours, till the beef starts offevolved to turn away from the bone.

Cool and shop the hocks of their cooking liquid till equipped to use. The braised hocks will maintain refrigerated for as much as four days.

PICNIC HAM

This little cured and cooked "ham" isn't always a ham at all: it's now no longer a reduce from the hind leg of the pig however instead from the shoulder or picnic. This instruction is much like that used for an Italian cooked ham, or prosciutto cotto: it's far brined in white wine,

covered with herbs, and lightly steamed withinside the oven. Slice the ham into steaks for eggs benedict or use it to make a outstanding rendition of Croque Monsieur.

MAKES 2 PICNIC HAMS, ABOUT I
POUND (450 G) EACH BRINE
I teaspoon black peppercorns
I teaspoon yellow mustard seeds
I teaspoon allspice berries
three entire
cloves I dried
bay leaf
7.2 ounces (two hundred grams) pleasant sea salt
10.four ounces (290 grams)
sugar 3½ quarts (three.three
L) boiling water I tablespoon
curing salt no. I
I½ cups (360 ml) dry white wine
2 boneless beef picnic roasts, I to I½ pounds (450 to 680 g) every
HERB RUB
I½ teaspoons freshly floor pepper
¼ cup (15 g) finely chopped sparkling flat-leaf parsley
¼ cup (15 g) finely chopped rosemary

¼ cup (15 g) finely chopped sage
2 tablespoons duck or beef gelée or broth(see Basic Rich Broth)

To make the brine, region the peppercorns, mustard seeds, allspice, cloves, and bay on a rectangular of cheesecloth, deliver the corners together, and tie securely with wire to make a sachet (or use a muslin bag). Place the ocean salt and sugar in a massive nonreactive box. Pour withinside the boiling water and stir to dissolve the salt and sugar. Add the sachet, cowl the box loosely, and permit cool for at the least four hours or for as much as in a single day, till cooled to room temperature.

Stir the curing salt and wine into the cooled brine. Using a brine pump, inject the middle of every picnic roast with approximately ¼ cup (60 ml)

Of the brine. Submerge the roasts withinside the last brine, pinnacle with a plate or different weight to preserve them submerged, and refrigerate for five days.

After five days, put off the hams from the brine. Truss them tightly into particularly uniform cylinders. Outfit a roasting pan with a rack. To make the herb rub, in a small bowl, integrate the pepper, parsley, rosemary, sage, and gelée and blend well. Coat the hams calmly with the aggregate and area at the rack.

Position an oven rack on the bottom rung withinside the oven after which role a 2nd rack withinside the top 1/3 of the oven. Preheat the oven to 200°F (95°C). Bring a small ovenproof saucepan packed with water to a boil at the range pinnacle and area the pan on the lowest rack.

Place the roasting pan protecting the hams at the top rack of the oven and prepare dinner dinner for forty five mins to one hour, till a thermometer inserted into the middle of every ham registers 140°F (60°C). Remove the hams from the oven and permit them to relaxation at room temperature for at the least 10 mins earlier than slicing.

If you'll be ingesting the hams bloodless or at a later date, do now no longer slice. Let them cool to room temperature, then wrap tightly in plastic wrap and refrigerate. They will preserve for up to ten days.

Croque Monsieur

CROQUE MONSIEUR

This Parisian café traditional can be the final ham and cheese sandwich: crisp, buttery, piled with salty, candy ham, and oozing with tacky Mornay sauce. Make it together along with your very own homecured ham for a unique treat.

SERVES FOUR
MORNAY SAUCE

1½ tablespoons unsalted butter

1½ tablespoons all-cause flour

1 cup (240 ml) entire milk

1 cup (115) grated Comté or Gruyère cheese

½ cup (fifty five g) grated Parmesan
cheese Pinch of freshly grated nutmeg
Pinch of floor cayenne Fine
sea salt
eight slices ache de mie or different good-first-class
sandwich bread 2 tablespoons unsalted butter, melted
I pound (450 g) boneless picnic ham, or different cured ham,
thinly sliced
½ cup (a hundred twenty five g) entire-grain mustard

To make the sauce, in a small saucepan, soften the butter over medium heat. Whisk withinside the flour till blended after which prepare dinner dinner and whisk for 1 minute. Slowly whisk withinside the milk, flip down the warmth to low, and prepare dinner dinner, stirring constantly, for approximately five mins, till clean and thick. Continue cooking and stirring for approximately five mins more, permitting the sauce to in addition thicken, then put off from the warmth and stir withinside the cheeses, nutmeg, and cayenne till the cheeses soften. Season with salt.

Preheat the oven to 450°F (230°C). Lay the bread slices in a unmarried layer on a baking sheet. Brush the slices with the butter, then turn them over, buttered aspect down. Spread the second one aspect of every slice with the mustard. Spoon 2 tablespoons of the Mornay sauce on pinnacle of every of four slices. Top the last four slices with one-fourth of the ham, observed via way of means of 1 tablespoon of the Mornay.

Place the baking sheet withinside the oven for eight to ten mins, till the sauce is effervescent and brown and the lowest of every bread slice is crisp and golden. Remove the pan from the oven and, the use of a spatula, marry every of the ham-crowned slices with a Mornay-crowned slice.

Serve immediately.

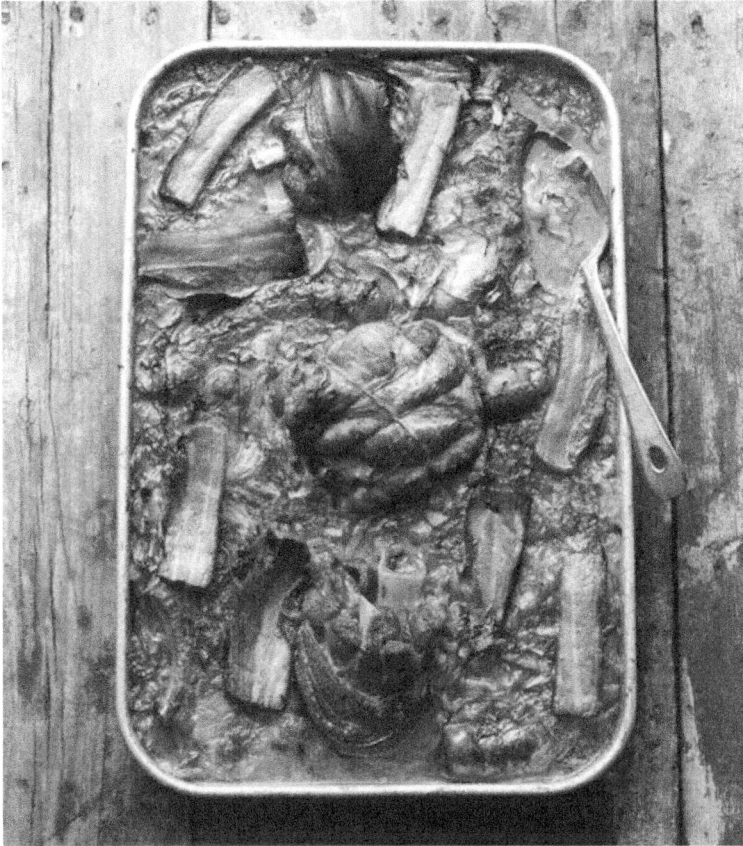

Choucroute Garni

CHOUCROUTE GARNI

This immensely hearty dish from France's borderland of Alsace is a traditional of charcuterie cooking. Brined, cured, and smoked meats and sausages are nestled in a mattress of tangy sauerkraut and braised in a mixture of smoky hock broth and bright, crisp Alsatian Riesling till tender. Although brining and smoking all the meats your self calls for considerable planning and prep work, the results are immensely satisfying. Serve with with boiled potatoes and lots of robust mustard.

SERVES EIGHT TO 10

¼ cup (fifty five g) rendered duck fats or drippings
1 boneless red meat shoulder roast, approximately 2 pounds
(900 g), brined in Garlic Brine
four Belgian Beer Sausage hyperlinks or
comparable sausage hyperlinks four raw Cider-
Brined Pork Porterhouse Chops 2 massive yellow
onions, thinly sliced
2 cups (480 ml) Alsatian Riesling or comparable
wine 2 Braised Ham Hocks with their braising
liquid
3 quarts (2.eight L) sauerkraut, home made or store-
sold 1 dried bay leaf
6 to eight juniper berries
2 entire cloves
eight thick slices bacon, home made or storebought

Preheat the oven to 300°F (150°C).

First, brown the meats. Set a 9- to ten-quart (eight.five to 9.five L) robust braiser over medium heat. Add the duck fats and warmth till pretty warm. Carefully region the brined beef shoulder withinside the pan and brown calmly on all sides. Transfer the roast to a huge platter and set aside. Add the hyperlinks and chops to the pan and brown calmly on each sides, then switch them to the platter with the shoulder roast.

Lower the heat, upload the onions to the pan, and prepare dinner dinner, stirring occasionally, for approximately eight to ten minutes, till smooth and translucent. Pour withinside the wine, carry to a simmer, and deglaze the pot, stirring with a timber spoon to loosen the fond from the lowest of the pot. Add the hocks and their braising liquid, the sauerkraut, and the bay, juniper, and cloves to the pot. Distribute the beef roast, hyperlinks, and chops calmly withinside the pan, tucking them into the sauerkraut. They need to be mainly covered, with simply a chunk peeking out from below the kraut. Lay the bacon slices throughout the pinnacle of the sauerkraut.

Cover the pot and region withinside the oven. Cook slowly for two hours, then find the pot and prepare dinner dinner for a further 30 to forty five minutes, till golden brown.

Remove the pot from the oven. Transfer the beef shoulder roast and the hyperlinks to a slicing board. Allow them to relaxation and funky for some minutes. Slice every sausage at the diagonal into four or five thick slices, then tuck the slices again into the sauerkraut. Cut the beef roast into slices and lay the slices on pinnacle of the sauerkraut. Serve at once from the pot on the table.

CORNED BEEF BRISKET

Corning is simply an old fashioned time period for salting or brining. The spice-encumbered brine infuses streaky pork brisket with the smelly flavors of mustard, coriander, juniper, and bay in a conventional prolonged soak. The ensuing corned pork may be simmered slowly in a conventional Irish American boiled supper, or rubbed with seasonings and smoked for the conventional deli favorite, Pastrami.

MAKES I CORNED BRISKET, ABOUT EIGHT POUNDS (THREE.6 KG)
I pound, 15 ounces (880 g) high-quality
sea salt I ¼ pounds (570 g) sugar
five teaspoons peppercorns
five teaspoons yellow mustard seeds
teaspoons coriander seeds
juniper berries
10 complete
cloves
three bay leaves
eleven quarts (10.four L) boiling water
¼ cup (seventy five g) curing salt no. I
I fatty pork brisket, approximately eight pounds (three.6 kg)

To make the brine, region the ocean salt, sugar, peppercorns, mustard seeds, coriander, juniper, cloves, and bay in a huge nonreactive field. Pour withinside the boiling water and stir to dissolve the salt and sugar. Cover the field loosely and permit cool absolutely overnight.

The subsequent day, stir the curing salt into the cooled brine.

Lightly rinse the brisket and pat dry. Using a brine pump, inject approximately ½ cup (one hundred twenty ml) of the brine into the middle of the brisket. Submerge the brisket withinside the ultimate brine, pinnacle with a plate or different weight to hold it submerged, and refrigerate for 10 days.

Remove the finished corned beef brisket from the brine and rinse well before cooking (see Cooking Corned Beef). Discard the brine.

COOKING CORNED BEEF

A complete brisket might also additionally look like a number of meat, however corned pork is the dish that maintains on giving. We continually prepare dinner dinner a corned pork two times as large as we suppose we would moderately want in hopes that the following day we are able to be capable of revel in a warm corned pork sandwich heaped with sauerkraut, caramelized onions, and Muenster cheese. Any stop bits may be shredded and saute'ed with onions, cooked beets, and potatoes for a hearty breakfast of pink flannel hash.

Choose a cooking pot this is wider and deeper than your hunk of pork is tall (you can want a deep roasting pan). Toss a coarsely chopped leek, more than one peeled complete carrots, a clove or or 3 of garlic; a stalk of celery, and a few sprigs of thyme and parsley. Set the corned pork brisket atop this fragrant mattress and cowl absolutely with bloodless water and possibly a beneficiant splash of beer. Place all of this in a preheated 300°F (150°C) oven and simmer for three to four hours. Prod the brisket with a meat fork to make sure it's miles gentle and yielding earlier than calling it quits. Let the beef relaxation in its cooking liquor for 20 to half-hour earlier than cautiously moving it to a carving board and cutting it towards the grain.

Seldom sticklers for tradition, we choose to prepare dinner dinner the desired cabbage and potatoes separately—or on occasion now no longer at all. (Sorry, Pop.) Boiled new potatoes with simply a chunk of butter and parsley will do, or a root

vegetable mash is good, too. Far better than long-boiled cabbage is chopped cabbage sautéed with bacon until just tender and finished with a ladleful of the braising liquor. Creamy horseradish sauce and some strong mustard round out this fine Irish American feast—a supper so good that you may need to ration a bit for the next day's sandwiches before you sit down.

Dry Curing

Curing meat is a apparently addictive hobby. It conjures up a sensation just like looking a lawn grow. You will want to do a piece of labor on the outset, however as soon as the preliminary exertions is done, there's most effective tending, waiting, prodding, and anticipation till the aroma peaks and the muscle feels ripe to the touch, equipped to reap. You may also revel in a sadness or at the same time as you're studying the ropes, however when you get the knack, you would possibly discover your self habitually smoking suitable golden slabs of bacon and stringing up spiced red meat jowls. It feels as proper and as enjoyable to tug down a completed pancetta because it does to reap plump pods of peas from the lawn.

Dry curing is a easy technique. A beneficiant layer of salt and different seasonings is rubbed onto the outdoor of a reduce of meat to each taste it and keep it. Similar to brining, dry curing is based on osmosis to attract the salt and seasonings into the beef and protein amendment to tenderize it. But not like brining, water isn't drawn in with the salt. Rather than including moisture to the beef, dry curing dehydrates it, pulling out extra water, concentrating the flavors, and turning the beef a deep, wealthy color.

Pork reigns superb withinside the global of dry curing. Although dry-cured hams, which includes the famed Italian prosciutto, are possibly the bestknown and maximum famous cured meats, almost each a part of the pig is a appropriate candidate for dry curing, from trotters and ears to bellies and loins. However, red meat isn't the most effective player. Cuts of duck, goose, beef, or even lamb may be dry cured, as properly.

Dry curing is normally one a part of a -component system. The preliminary dry remedy starts whilst the beef is salted and moisture is authorized to drain

off. This first component can take everywhere from some days to 3 weeks. Once the beef has misplaced the bulk of its moisture, it may be both smoked or air-dried. Meats which are completed with smoke normally require much less of an preliminary dry remedy due to the fact smoking attracts out extra moisture and affords a further layer of preservation. Airdried meats require an extended preliminary dry remedy, and then they have to be hung in a fab area to remedy and company up completely sufficient to devour with out cooking. They can dangle everywhere from some weeks for smaller cuts, which includes Guanciale, to multiple years for a cured ham.

Ingredients for Dry Curing

Dry curing includes a acquainted solid of characters.

Salt affords taste, modifications the feel with the aid of using drawing out moisture, slows the boom of micro organism the usage of dehydration, and regulates the fermentation system with the aid of using decreasing the water pastime level. We use a best sea salt for dry curing due to the fact it's miles maximum quite simply absorbed with the aid of using the beef.

Curing salt is nearly usually utilized in dry curing as it preserve meats from spoiling and, maximum importantly, it inhibits the boom of botulism. See greater data on the 2 number one forms of curing salt.

Sugar is from time to time used for flavoring and to assist to stability saltiness. Any wide variety of sugars or sweeteners may be used, from easy cane sugar to maple syrup to honey. Dextrose is a famous preference for drycured meats due to the fact it's miles finely textured, without problems absorbed, and has a much less mentioned sweetness. Sugars additionally offer meals for micro organism instrumental to the fermentation system.

Aromatics which includes spices, dried herbs, garlic, and wine also can be used to impart plenty of diffused flavors on your cured meat.

Dry-Curing Basics

1. Gather your device and make certain you've got got sufficient area for refrigeration or every other cool area to save your meat all through the dry-curing system. Choose a box this is product of tough foodgrade plastic or different nonreactive material. It have to be at

least a touch large than the reduce of meat you may be curing. For a few drycured items, you may additionally want a huge plastic colander for draining all through the preliminary remedy. Restaurant deliver shops frequently promote meals-grade plastic pans or packing containers with perforated inserts which are best for dry curing and properly really well worth the small investment.

2. Prepare the dry-remedy blend. Carefully degree and integrate the ocean salt, curing salt, sugar, and aromatics, then blend properly to distribute the components evenly.

3. Trim and weigh the beef to calculate the quantity of dry-treatment blend you may want. Be positive to take away any silver pores and skin or glands very well and trim the beef right into a really neat or uniform form earlier than weighing it. The quantity of dry-treatment blend you may want is calculated in step with the load of the beef, and is normally approximately three percentage of the load of the beef to be air-dried. This rule does now no longer follow to meats as a way to be completed with the aid of using warm smoking or cooking.

4. Perforate the beef with the aid of using piercing its floor very well and flippantly with the tines of a sausage knife, the sharp quit of a trussing needle, or a pointy skewer. The perforations permit the dry-treatment blend to be greater effortlessly absorbed.

5. Rub the beef with the dry-treatment blend, then rubdown the combinationture into the beef in order that it penetrates very well.

6. Let the dry curing begin. Place the rubbed meat into the selected box. Label, date, and refrigerate the box. Drain off extra liquid and rotate as needed. The meat will lose maximum of its liquid withinside the first few days after which the system will slow.

7. Finish the curing system with the aid of using air-drying or smoking. After the preliminary dry curing, maximum cured meats are completed both with the aid of using smoking or with the aid of using striking for air-drying. Meats which are air-dried need to be saved pretty cool, generally at approximately 50°F (10°C).

Oftentimes a mild mildew will shape at the out of doors of the beef because it ages. In maximum cases, this is

useful in preference to harmful, growing a barrier that enables to defend the beef towards probably risky pathogens for the duration of the drying system.

Pancetta Arrotolata

PANCETTA ARROTOLATA

Pancetta is a sort of cured beef stomach, however not like its candy and smoky American cousin, bacon, Italian pancetta is air-dried after its preliminary treatment. There are primary sorts of pancetta, *tesa and arrotolata. Pancetta tesa is a flat pancetta*, dried in its herbal form till it's so company and dry that it could be eaten raw

like prosciutto. *Pancetta arrotolata is rolled*, trussed, and cured till simply company. Sliced or diced, it's miles the cured meat workhorse of the Italian kitchen, locating its manner into tortellini and onto pizza, lending its delicately candy porkiness to sughi, *insalate, zuppe*, and verdure, and barding lean meats together with beef tenderloin with its sufficient fats, retaining them juicy and scrumptious for the duration of roasting.

Start to finish, this pancetta will take not less than four weeks to put together and treatment. If you decide upon a totally company pancetta, you may hold to allow it dangle for numerous greater weeks.

MAKES ABOUT ONE 6½-POUND (THREE-KG) ROLLED PANCETTA
I skinless, boneless beef stomach, approximately eight pounds (three.6 kg) or barely larger
CURE MIX
I tablespoon black peppercorns
2 teaspoons chile flakes
I dried bay leaf
five allspice
berries
three ounces (eighty five g) first-
class sea salt tablespoon dextrose
teaspoons curing salt no. 2
¼ teaspoon freshly grated nutmeg

Trim and rectangular off the beef stomach in order that it weighs approximately eight pounds (three.6 kg), provide or take 1 ounce (30 g). (Any trim may be stored for sausage or rillettes.) Lay the stomach fats aspect down on a reducing board and pierce with the tines of a sausage knife, the sharp quit of a trussing needle, or a pointy skewer, protecting it absolutely with perforations kind of ½ inch (12 mm) apart.

To make the treatment blend, in a spice grinder, integrate the peppercorns, chile flakes, bay leaf, and allspice and grind finely. Transfer to a small bowl, upload the ocean salt, dextrose, curing salt, and nutmeg, and blend nicely to distribute the components flippantly.

Place the beef stomach in a nonreactive pan or box big sufficient to maintain it flat. Rub the treatment throughout each aspects and all of the rims of the stomach, ensuring to paintings the treatment in among any crevices. When all the treatment has been massaged into the beef, lay the stomach fats aspect down withinside the box, cover, and refrigerate.

The following day, turn the stomach over so the fats aspect faces up. Turn it over again the next day in order that the fats aspect over again faces down. Recover it, go back it to the refrigerator, and go away it undisturbed to treatment for every other 12 days.

Remove the stomach from the pan. Using a meat hook, dangle the stomach withinside the refrigerator (or different bloodless location) for two days to dry further. Place a pan or shallow bowl under the stomach to trap any dripping juices.

When the stomach is dry, put off it from the fridge and allow it take a seat down at room temperature for approximately three hours, till it's far gentle and malleable. Cover a huge reducing board with plastic wrap. Lay the tempered stomach, meaty aspect up, on pinnacle of the plastic wrap. Place some other layer of plastic wrap on pinnacle of the stomach. Using a heavy meat tenderizer, rubber mallet, or rolling pin, pound the pancetta very well, lightly, and with out mercy for a complete five minutes, till it's far extra pliable and smooth to roll.

To roll and tie the pancetta, lay the stomach, meaty aspect up, with its longest aspect closest to you. Starting on the aspect closest to you, fold the primary 2 inches (five cm) over onto themselves and press down firmly. Continue to roll and press, ensuring to put off any air gaps which can bring about undesirable mould at the inner of the pancetta. When the stomach is absolutely rolled, tie it with butcher's cord as you will a roast (see How to Tie a Roast), tying it as tightly as feasible, then rehang it withinside the fridge for some other 2 weeks or till it's far organization in your liking.

Pancetta maintains exceptional while left complete or in huge pieces. Slice off best what's to be cooked and tightly wrap the unused element in plastic wrap. It will hold properly withinside the fridge for three to four weeks or withinside the freezer for up to six months.

BRESAOLA

Bresaola is a northern Italian dry-cured uniqueness made with lean pork eye of spherical. Dry curing tenderizes this regularly hard reduce and complements its rich, beefy taste. We choose to case the attention of spherical in pork caps earlier than hanging. Beef fats is extra at risk of spoilage than pork, and the cap protects towards spoilage because it airdries. It additionally offers the attention of spherical a neat and uniform shape, making sure a extra even dry treatment. Thinly sliced, *bresaola is a lovely deep pink and has an earthy taste that may be loved both as a part of an diverse antipasto or tossed right into a salad of sour greens,* persimmons, olives, and pecorino cheese.

MAKES ABOUT THREE POUNDS (I.FOUR KG) CURE MIX
I ½ teaspoons peppercorns
½ teaspoon coriander seeds
2 allspice berries
2 juniper berries
I complete clove
I¾ ounces (50 grams) pleasant sea salt 2 teaspoons curing salt no.2 I (four-pound/1.8-kg) pork eye of spherical, absolutely trimmed of all outside fats and silver skin
I pork cap, rinsed and grew to become inner out

To make the treatment blend, in a spice grinder, integrate the peppercorns, coriander, allspice, juniper, and clove and grind finely. Transfer to a small bowl, upload the ocean salt and curing salt, and blend properly to distribute the substances lightly.

Check the attention of spherical cautiously to ensure it's far trimmed of all outside fats and silver skin. Pierce the floor of the attention of spherical very well and lightly with the tines of a sausage knife, the sharp quit of a trussing needle, or a pointy skewer, overlaying it absolutely with perforations more or less ½ inch (12 mm) apart.

Lay the attention of spherical in a huge, flat nonreactive field (a huge ceramic baking dish or food-grade plastic garage field works properly). Rub the treatment blend lightly over the floor of the pork, massaging it in properly. Cover the field loosely and refrigerate overnight.

The subsequent day, baste the pork with the liquid that has amassed withinside the field. Place the attention of spherical right into a huge plastic colander or drain pan set over a field. Cover and refrigerate. Every day for two weeks, flip the pork withinside the colander and discard any amassed drippings.

After 2 weeks, case the attention of spherical withinside the pork cap. Remove the attention of spherical from the fridge. Drain off any extra water from the rinsed pork cap. Roll the open quit of the pork cap onto one quit of the attention of spherical, then pull it completely over the meat, like a sock over a foot. Pull it taut and clean out any air wallet. Using butcher's cord, and starting on the closed quit, tie the encased eye of spherical with butcher's cord as you will a roast (see How to Tie a Roast), tying it as tightly as feasible and urgent out any air wallet which could shape as you go. Tie a knot and loop on the open quit of the pork cap, as you will for salami (see Casing, Linking, Looping, and Tying). Hang the cased meat in a cool, dry location (50°F/10°C is optimal) for six to eight weeks. It is prepared while it feels organization, like a properly-executed roast.

To serve, peel returned the casing at the component you intend on slicing. Slice crosswise as thinly as viable into rounds, ideally the use of a meat slicer. *Bresaola is pleasant while freshly sliced and served proper away*, because it has an inclination to oxidize and dry out extra quick than different cured meats. Tightly wrap the unused component in plastic wrap. It will hold nicely withinside the fridge for 1 to two months.

GUANCIALE

Guanciale

Guancia is Italian for "cheek," and guanciale, a area of expertise of critical Italy, is cured beef jowl that has been rubbed with an fragrant mixture of black pepper, warm chile, and dried rosemary. Although it may be utilized in the various equal methods that pancetta is used, *guanciale simply has a persona all its own.* When slowly crisped in a pan, it offers off an intriguing, spicy, sharp perfume that awakens the hunger. Sauté skinny shards of guanciale with peas, asparagus, and spring onions, or toss crispy bits of sautéed guanciale with shredded Lacinato kale, pecOrino cheese, plumped currants, and toasted pine nuts for a fulfilling salad. Or, use it because the Romans do, for a sturdy bowl of bucatini all'amatriciana or spaghetti alla carbonara.

MAKES THREE TO FOUR POUNDS (I.FOUR TO I.EIGHT KG)
five pounds (2.three kg) pores and skin-on beef jowls
CURE MIX
I teaspoons black peppercorns
2 teaspoons chile flakes
I teaspoon dried oregano
½ teaspoon aniseeds, toasted
I dried bay leaf
2 ounces (fifty five grams)
quality sea salt 2 teaspoons
curing salt no.2
RUB
2 tablespoons coarsely chopped driedrosemary
three tablespoons finely floor chile flakes
¼ cup (28 g) freshly floor pepper

Trim the jowls of all glands. The glands generally tend to live at the internal meaty facet of the jowls and are distinguishable via way of means of their off-white, bright appearance. Shave away any ragged edges in order that the jowls have a extremely uniform appearance. Prick the beef facet of the jowls with the tines of a sausage knife, the sharp stop of a trussing needle or a pointy skewer, overlaying it absolutely with perforations kind of ½ inch (12 mm) aside. Leave the pores and skin facet undisturbed.

To make the therapy blend, in a spice grinder, integrate the peppercorns, chile flakes, bay leaf, oregano, aniseeds, and bay and grind finely. Transfer to a small bowl, upload the ocean salt and curing salt, and blend nicely to distribute the substances calmly.

Rub the therapy blend onto all aspects of the jowls, area in a nonreactive container (it's miles quality if the jowls are stacked or touching), and refrigerate. Every day for two weeks, blend the jowls and rotate the jowls on the lowest to the pinnacle to make sure that the therapy is calmly penetrating every jowl.

After 2 weeks, get rid of the jowls from the fridge. Using a trussing needle and butcher's cord, pierce the pinnacle of every jowl and run the cord via to create a loop. Hang the jowls in a dry, cool location (50°F/10°C is optimal) to therapy. Be positive to area the jowls as a minimum three inches (7.five cm) aside to permit for correct airflow. After kind of three weeks, the jowls need to sense pretty organization and may be taken down.

To make the rub, in a small bowl, integrate the rosemary, chile flakes, and pepper and blend nicely. Massage the rub into the beef facet of every jowl. Wrap every jowl in plastic and refrigerate. Allow the rubbed jowls to take a seat down in a single day to permit the flavors of the rub to marry with the beef earlier than the use of.

The guanciale may be sliced with its pOres and skin intact in case you experience the chewy texture. Or, you could peel away the pores and skin with a pointy knife earlier than slicing. If you do peel off the pores and skin, store it and toss it into your subsequent pot of beans or minestrone to feature complexity. Slice best what you want on the time, then tightly wrap the unused component in plastic wrap. It will hold nicely withinside the fridge for four to six weeks or withinside the freezer for up to six months.

Brown Sugar–Cured Bacon

BROWN SUGAR–CURED BACON

A slab of bacon simply out of the smoker is heaven on a platter. It is difficult to face up to tearing off a touch stop piece and shoving the still-steaming, salty, candy meat into your mouth. Most commercially produced bacon is brined (or brine injected), however dry curing it—as we propose on this recipe—produces meatier and extra flavorful bacon that won't spit and curl while you prepare dinner dinner it. Choose beef bellies which might be pretty thick, with a reasonably same lean to fats ratio, maintaining in thoughts that they'll reduce barely throughout the curing and smoking process. This a notably brief dry-curing project, requiring simply three days.

MAKES 2 SLABS, ABOUT 3½ POUNDS (1.6 KG) EACH
1 entire thick boneless, skinless beef stomach, approximately eight pounds (three.6 kg)
CURE MIX
1 pound (450 g) brown sugar
12 ounces (340 g) first-class
sea salt 1 tablespoon curing
salt no. 1 1 tablespoon floor
cayenne
1 tablespoon freshly floor black pepper

Use a pointy knife to rectangular off the rims of the beef stomach, then reduce in 1/2 of crosswise to yield a couple of especially rectangular portions of approximately the equal size. Be certain to store any stomach trim for sausage or rillettes or different potted meats.

To make the therapy blend, in a bowl, integrate the brown sugar, sea salt, curing salt, cayenne, and black pepper.

Spread approximately 1 cup (250 g) of the therapy blend frivolously over the lowest of a box huge sufficient to house the stomach squares, one stacked on pinnacle of the different. Place a stomach 1/2 of, meat aspect down, immediately on pinnacle of the therapy.

Rub an extra 1 cup (250 g) of the therapy on the rims and fats aspect of the stomach, ensuring to get the combinationture into all of

the crevices. Place the second one rectangular of stomach, meat aspect down, on pinnacle of the first. Rub any other 1 cup (250 g) of the combinationture on the rims and fats aspect of the stomach, once more ensuring to get the combinationture into all the crevices. Cover loosely and refrigerate overnight.

The following day, put off the stomach slabs from the box and pour off any gathered liquid. Switch the location of the slabs, putting the slab formerly on pinnacle on the lowest of the box and the lowest slab on pinnacle. Rub any closing therapy blend everywhere that it is probably lacking. Re-cowl and go back to the fridge for any other 24 hours. The following day, rotate the slabs once more.

After the stomach slabs have cured for three complete days, put off them from the pan and rinse them speedy below heat strolling water to put off any solids. Pat the slabs dry.

Prepare your smokehouse, following the hints indexed for Hot and Cold Smoking, and warmth to 160°F to 180°F (70°C to 82°C). Place the stomach slabs on a rack withinside the smoker and smoke for two to a few hours, till a thermometer inserted into the middle of a slab registers 140°F (60°C).

Remove the bacon from the smoker and allow it cool to room temperature, then refrigerate. The bacon ought to be properly chilled earlier than slicing.

Publisher 1st baron verulam maintains quality in slab form. Slice simplest what you want on the time, then tightly wrap the unused component in plastic wrap. It will preserve properly withinside the fridge for two to a few weeks or withinside the freezer for up to six months.

Finishing with Smoke

What primeval yen attracts us to the fire? The captivating fragrance of wooden smoke appears to beckon us outside to acquire across the outdoor barbeque and undergo witness to the electricity of succulent smoked meats. The promise of a gentle rack of spareribs or a chunk of pork brisket immediately out of the smoker is sufficient to make you overlook simply how realistic smoking definitely is.

Smoke has lengthy been used as a technique of meat protection in cultures across the world. Wood smoke evidently slows the increase of

dangerous organisms. Phenolic compounds and formaldehyde contained in smoke are antimicrobial. Plus, smoke emits acids that create a protecting layer at the out of doors of the beef that forestalls the increase of floor mildew and micro organism that could purpose rancidity. Smoke additionally lowers the pH degree at the floor of the beef, in addition discouraging the increase of dangerous organisms. Used along with brining or dry curing, smoking has the capacity to hold meat for weeks, months, or maybe years.

The equal phenols, carbonyl compounds, and natural acids that guard and hold the beef additionally imbue it with an impossible to resist taste. Refrigeration and different present day protection techniques have rendered smoking unnecessary, however the taste of smoke has a intensity and richness this is unparalleled. We retain to smoke our meals due to the fact we adore the flavor that it offers them. Smoking meat has grow to be a craft that we exercise for the natural pleasure it brings us.

The Smokehouse

Much ado is made approximately people who smoke, and there are a few quite spendy people who smoke available in the marketplace those days. But the smoker, at its maximum rudimentary, is virtually only a container with an inner or an connected heatsmoke supply and a chimney that allows to manipulate the draft of smoke. It is the beef you install it, the wooden you operate to smoke it, and the care you supply it that make the completed product tremendous. Choosing the smoker this is proper for you and your desires is a private choice in an effort to depend upon your frequency of usage, the overall portions of gadgets you need to smoke, your to be had area and environment, and your budget. You might also additionally locate that there are a few bells and whistles which you need to have and others that you could do without. That said, right here are some fundamental capabilities to consider.

Control Yourself: A thermostat or dampers that let you manipulate the draft is crucial for controlling the temperature of the smoker. A thermometer to take the ambient temperature of the interior of the smoker and a probe thermometer to take the inner temperature of the beef also are necessary.

Hang Ups: You will want hooks and bars, racks, or monitors to cling or relaxation the beef on. Stainless metallic is usually an excellent preference for hardware, as it's miles sturdy, cleans up easily, and resists rusting.

Just Add Water: Regulating humidity withinside the smoke chamber allows to preserve the beef wet throughout. Cold smoking commonly calls for a humidity degree of approximately seventy five percent. The humidity degree for warm smoking normally tiers from 50 to 60 percent. Humidity sensors or meters are accessible that will help you to gauge the want for extra or much less humidity. To upload humidity to the smoke chamber, use a water pan (a few people who smoke come ready with a water pan, however you could additionally definitely fill a pan with water and area it withinside the smoker). Soaking wooden or wooden chips for the hearthplace additionally allows to create a extra humid environment.

GASSTINKS

Mercaptans are the stinky organic compounds redolent of rotten eggs, decomposing cabbage, or bad breath that are added to propane and natural gas. They are highly detectable, even at only a few parts per million, which is exactly why they are used in odorless gas and propane. They immediately signal the possibility of a hazardous leak to the human nose. Although they serve a valuable function, food exposed to mercapatans can pick up unwanted bitter or unpleasant flavors. Stick to charcoal, electric, or allwood-fired smokers to avoid the stink.

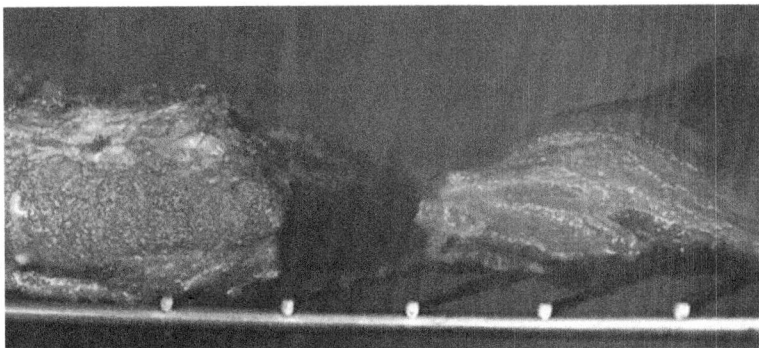

The Woodpile

All herbal hardwoods and fruitwoods can infuse your meat with a selection of various aromas. Each wooden creates a completely unique smoke and taste.

Alder is a dependable fundamental wooden with a herbal, diffused sweetness and sensitive taste that works properly whilst combined with different, extra nuanced woods, which include apple or cherry.

Almond is a clean-burning wooden which can create an excellent little bit of heat, making it incredible for beginning a hearthplace and developing a mattress of coals to which you could upload different fragrant woods.

Apple imparts a candy and faintly fruity aroma this is ideal for bacon, ham, and red meat chops however slight sufficient for rooster as properly.

Cherry provides a light, candy taste whilst combined with extra strongly flavored woods which include alder, oak, or hickory.

Grapevines have a one of a kind taste that works properly with recreation birds. They are ideal for including brief bursts of warmth or a brief infusion of smoke whilst grilling, however now no longer tremendous for longer smoke periods, as they normally burn quickly.

Hickory offers a sturdy and smelly smoky taste this is traditional for smoking pork however regularly too severe for extra delicately flavored meats. Maple has a candy and sensitive aroma and is great mixed with oak, apple, or alder for smoking hams, bacon, or birds.

Mesquite is oily, burns warm, and has an severe and every so often overpowering taste. It is great utilized in tandem with different kinds of wooden.

Oak is the standard, all-cause preference, closely preferred through opposition fish fry peoples for its truthful taste. Although it may burn warm however due to the fact it's miles very dense, it's going to additionally burn slowly, making it most desirable for smoking massive cuts.

Pecan is sort of a milder model of hickory. It burns slowly and at a decrease temperature than maximum woods, however its fruity smoke is smelly and is great utilized in moderation.

Hot and Cold Smoking

There are kinds of smoking: bloodless and warm. Cold smoking is used to taste the beef as opposed to prepare dinner dinner it. The meat is positioned in an unheated chamber and the smoke is funneled in from a firebox. Smokehouse temperatures for bloodless smoking ought to be underneath 100°F (38°C). Wood dust, chips, or pellets paintings great for bloodless smoking, as they'll smolder and smoke at a decrease temperature. Hot smoking is corresponding to sluggish roasting with the addition of aromatic smoke and is used to prepare dinner dinner the beef thoroughly. Smokehouse temperatures for warm smoking variety from approximately 160°F to 185°F (70°C to 85°C).

Smoking Basics

1. Fat is your friend. The herbal layer of subcutaneous fats at the outdoor of the beef in addition to the adequate intramuscular fats or marbling will assist to preserve the beef wet and flavorful at some stage in its long, sluggish smoke.

2. Form the pellicle. Before your brined, dry-cured, or pro meats set foot withinside the smoker, they want to be air-dried in order that they shape a pellicle, a cheesy coating of proteins at the floor of meat that permits smoke to higher adhere to the floor. Air-dry the meats exposed withinside the fridge, ideally on a rack or striking from a hook to make sure they dry absolutely and lightly.

3. Remove any lingering ash. Make certain you get rid of the ash from the preceding smoking consultation earlier than you smoke.

4. Gloves are good. Heavy, nonflammable paintings gloves are outstanding for shielding your digits whilst futzing with the hearthplace and poking round withinside the smokehouse.

5. Light your hearthplace naturally. Avoid the use of lighter fluid or another chemical merchandise that would produce unsightly flavors.

6. Let your coals burn down. Before you region meat in the smokehouse, allow you to coals burn right all the way down to the right temperature.

7. Start your meat fats aspect up. As the fats starts to melt, it'll baste the beef, preserving it juicy.

8. Slow and occasional is the pit master's mantra. There need to be no flames, no flare-ups, and no sizzle at any point. If you do have a flare-up or if the smokehouse receives too hot, get rid of the beef and permit matters cool off earlier than continuing. Smoking at too excessive of a temperature will dry out your meat and decrease your yield.

9. Use thermometers. You want one thermometer to screen the ambient temperature of the smokehouse, and a 2d one to maintain music of the inner temperature of the beef. Even in case your smoked meats are properly cooked and have been made with out curing salt, they'll frequently have a rosy interior. Sometimes (in case you're lucky) they'll have a vibrant crimson ring round their exterior, the coveted smoke ring this is the Holy Grail of barbeque enthusiasts.

10. Let it relaxation. As with many cooked meats, permit your smoked meat relaxation for as a minimum 10 to fifteen mins earlier than reducing and serving.

PASTRAMI

Pastrami

Pastrami is a undertaking properly really well worth the effort. One chunk of this smoky, highly spiced brisket and you would possibly by no means slum it on the grocery store again. Some conventional pastrami recipes name for steaming the beef similarly to smoking, however on this model the steaming and smoking take place simultaneously, ensuing in a meltingly soft brisket, geared up to slice and heap onto strong rye bread.

MAKES I WHOLE PASTRAMI, ABOUT EIGHT POUNDS (THREE.6 KG)

Corned Beef Brisket

SPICE MIX

½ cup (forty g) coriander seeds, toasted

¼ cup (35 g) peppercorns

1 tablespoon cumin seeds, toasted

¼ cup (forty g) yellow mustard seeds

½ cup (fifty five g) Spanish unsmoked

paprika 1½ teaspoons floor cayenne

¼ cup (fifty five g) firmly packed brown sugar

Pat the brisket with paper towels to get rid of any extra moisture and permit it to air-dry at room temperature for approximately 1 hour. Place the brisket on a huge baking sheet.

To make the spice mix, in a spice grinder, integrate the coriander, peppercorns, cumin, and mustard seeds. Transfer to a small bowl, upload the paprika, cayenne, and sugar, and blend properly to distribute the elements lightly.

Cover the brisket lightly with the spice mix, patting it on instead thickly. Refrigerate exposed overnight.

The following day, put together your smokehouse, following the tips indexed for Hot and Cold Smoking, and warmth to approximately 165°F (75°C). If your smoker is ready with a water pan, fill it. If not, fill a Dutch oven with water, carry to a rolling boil at the range top, after which cautiously region it withinside the backside of the cupboard or immediately withinside the coals, relying at the layout of your smoker. This regulates the temperature and facilitates to create steam to maintain the brisket wet and soft. Place the brisket withinside the smoker. Tend to the hearthplace and keep a regular temperature as needed.

Smoke the brisket for approximately three hours, till a thermometer inserted into the middle registers approximately 150°F (65°C).

Let the brisket relaxation for as a minimum half-hour earlier than reducing and serving, or permit cool absolutely to room temperature earlier than wrapping tightly in plastic wrap and refrigerating in case you choose to experience it cold. It will maintain properly withinside the fridge for up to two weeks.

Pulled Pork

PULLED PORK

We can think about few higher approaches to spend a lazy summer time season day than to slowly smoke a red meat shoulder to soft perfection after which shred it little by little right into a steaming, impossible to resist mess. And there are few higher approaches to feed a crowd than with a multitude of pulled red meat.

Traditionalists and keepers of the barbeque flame want to recognize that this recipe does now no longer declare to ascribe to a selected style, put on any pedigree of authenticity, or assignment the loved recipe of your grandpa. But it's far pretty tasty and really well worth a pass even for the pro pit master. The brine starts offevolved tenderizing the beef and the long, leisurely smoke finishes the job. When all is stated and done, this shoulder need to be so gentle it nearly shreds itself.

MAKES A MESS OF PULLED PORK, ENOUGH TO SERVE 10 TO 12
1 skinless, boneless beef picnic shoulder, butterflied and soaked in Garlic Brine for three days
Black Coffee and Bourbon Barbecue Sauce

Line a baking sheet with a kitchen towel. Remove the beef from the brine, area it at the organized baking sheet, and refrigerate exposed in a single day to dry.

The following day, put together your smokehouse, following the recommendations indexed for Hot and Cold Smoking, and warmth to approximately to 180°F (82°C). Place the picnic on a rack withinside the smoker. Open the picnic up absolutely to show a most of floor area. Put a pan under the rack to seize any drippings that gather because the picnic cooks. Tend to the hearthplace and preserve a regular temperature as wished.

Slowly smoke the picnic for approximately four hours (a ways past well-done), till a thermometer inserted into the thickest a part of the beef registers 175°F (80°C). The connective tissue can have nearly collapsed and the beef can be gentle and obscenely flavorful.

Remove the picnic from the smoker and set it on a tray to rest. When it's far cool sufficient to handle, spoil it aside into chunks approximately the scale of your thumb. Place the beef in a pot and stir in sufficient of the barbeque sauce and the drippings to coat the beef well. Place over very low warmness and hold at a naked simmer for 30 mins, till the beef absorbs the sauce. Taste for seasoning and upload extra sauce as desired, then serve.

Cowboy Beans

FIVE

ACCOUTREMENTS

One can not subsist on

meat alone. At the Fatted Calf, we provide all

way of seasonal pickles and preserves, mustards and chutneys, crunchy veggies and hearty legumes to accompany our roasts, pâtés, salami, and smoked and cured meats. Served atop a sandwich, along a sausage or spooned over grilled meats, those accoutrements serve to offer stability to the wealthy flavors of charcuterie.

BREAD AND BUTTER PICKLES

At the Fatted Calf, we make bucketsful of those pickles in the course of cucumber season. A little much less candy and a bit extra piquant than conventional bread and butter pickles, they're a extremely good addition to burgers, an high-quality accompaniment to smoked meats, and a welcome thing of any charcuterie spread. You will locate countless excuses to consume them with meaty items or all through their crunchy, sweetly spiced selves. A jar of those impossible to resist chips in no way lasts long, that's why this recipe makes 3 jars. Choose cucumbers which can be firm, vivid green, and no extra than five inches (12 cm) long.

MAKES ABOUT THREE QUART(THREE L) JARS
four pounds (1.eight kg) pickling cucumbers
6 cups (1.four L) cider vinegar, plus extra if
wished 3½ cups (660 g) firmly packed darkish
brown sugar
¼ cup (70 g) first-class sea salt
1½ tablespoons yellow mustard seeds
½ teaspoon allspice berries
1 teaspoon celery seeds
½ teaspoon floor turmeric 1
yellow onion, diced
1 crimson candy pepper, seeded and
diced 6 cloves garlic, gently crushed
three dried cayenne chiles

To put together the cucumbers, area them in a massive container, upload bloodless water to cover, and allow soak for 30 mins. Remove from the water, trim away any remnants from the blossom ends, and make certain the cucumbers are squeaky clean. Drain the wiped clean cucumbers in a colander.

Using a mandoline or a pointy knife, slice the cucumbers into chips approximately ⅛ inch (three mm) thick. Divide the cucumbers flippantly amongst three sterilized quart (or liter) canning jars.

To make the brine, in a saucepan, convey the 6 cups (1.four L) vinegar to a speedy simmer over excessive warmness. Add the sugar and salt and stir to dissolve, then decrease the warmth to medium. Add the mustard seeds, allspice, celery seeds, turmeric, onion, candy pepper, garlic, and chiles and simmer for approximately five mins to permit the flavors to commingle.

Carefully ladle the brine over the cucumbers, dispensing the seasonings as lightly as possible. Make positive the cucumbers are submerged withinside the brine. Top the jars with extra vinegar if necessary, permitting approximately ½ inch (12 mm) headspace, then lid the jars tightly. After the jars have cooled sufficient to handle, flip them the wrong way up and hold to chill absolutely to room temperature. Place upright withinside the fridge.

Let the pickles take a seat down withinside the fridge for some days earlier than consuming to permit their flavors to meld. They will preserve withinside the fridge for four to six weeks. If you pick longer storage, technique the lidded jars in a hotwater tubtub.

WATER BATH CANNING

Canning pickles and preserves ensures a prepared deliver of your favored accompaniments year-round. The maximum common, safest, and best approach is water-tubtub canning. Just region your chutney, *mostarda*, or pickles into sterilized glass jars and submerge them in a pot of simmering water to prepare dinner dinner, or "technique." As the jars prepare dinner dinner withinside the water, their contents create steam that presses in opposition to the lid of the jar and forces air out of the headspace. When the jars have completed processing and they're left to chill, the steam condenses into water, leaving a vacuum that tugs inward at the lid, sealing the jar and growing the function canning pop.

To technique your selfmade pickles and preserves, you may want a pot equipped with a rack and glass canning jars with lids. Traditional canning pots have a specifically equipped canning rack and are surprisingly recommended. A jar lifter and a canning funnel also are handy.

1. Start easy. Make positive all your cookingimplements and paintings surfaces are easy to keep away from any contamination.
2. Check your jars for any nicks or cracks. Suchimperfections can harbor bacteria, and any fractures to your jars are in all likelihood to rupture all through the water-tubtub processing. If you're the usage of glass jars with lids and screw-on bands, the jars and bands are reusable if they're in suitable condition, however the lids have to be used handiest as soon as for safety.
3. Sterilize your canning jars and lids both byrunning them via the dishwasher or through washing them with hot, soapy water and rinsing them with boiling water.
4. Set the jars apart in a heat region whilst youprepare your pickles, chutney, sauce, or mostarda.
5. Fill a canning pot a bit extra than 1/2 of complete withwater and produce to a energetic simmer.
6. Fill the jars, leaving a bit area among thecontents and the rim—that is the headspace—to permit for enlargement all through processing. About ½ inch (12 mm) is standard.
7. Wipe the edges of the jars easy and seal the jarswith their lids. Be cautious now no longer to

overtighten the lids, as air wishes if you want to get away all through processing.

8. Place the jars in a canning rack and decrease theminto the water. Make positive the tops of the jars are protected with water through at the least 1 inch (2.five cm).

9. Lid the pot and flip up the warmth to carry thewater to a boil.

10. Once the water is boiling, set a timer. Wegenerally technique pint (480 ml) jars for 20 to twenty-five mins and quart (liter) jars for 30 to 35 mins.

11. Turn off the warmth and allow the jars take a seat down withinside the waterbath for five mins. Lay a dish towel in your countertop. Carefully eliminate the jars from the pot, region at the towel, and go away undisturbed for approximately 12 hours.

12. Check every jar to make certain it's far properlysealed: If the lid is concave and does now no longer deliver whilst pressed, the seal is suitable. If the lid actions up and down, the seal failed and the jar must be saved withinside the fridge.

Properly sealed jars can be stored in a cool cupboard for up to a year. Once open, store refrigerated.

CLASSIC CUCUMBER DILLS

Unlike maximum pickles, which might be made with a vinegar-primarily based totally brine, the sourness of those pickles is derived from the fermentation technique. Fermentation may be unpredictable, though, and over time we began out including a small quantity of vinegar to behave as a catalyst and regulator, generating a totally steady dill pickle. When selecting your percent of pickling cucumbers, you'll want to be choosy. The nice and freshness of the cucumbers is of extreme significance on this recipe. Pick firm, incredibly small (someplace round four inches/10 cm long), lightly shaped pickling cucumbers without bruising or abrasions, ideally with the stem quit intact. Grape leaves, wealthy in tannins, assist to hold the cucumbers' crunchy nice.

MAKES ABOUT FOUR QUART (FOUR L) JARS
eight cups (2 L) warm water
¼ cup (70 g) best sea salt
½ cup (one hundred twenty ml) white wine vinegar
four pounds (1.eight kg) very clean pickling cucumbers
½ teaspoon yellow mustard seeds
1 teaspoon peppercorns
1½ teaspoons coriander seeds
2 allspice berries
1 dried bay leaf
1 dried cayenne chile
three cloves garlic, gently crushed
Several sprigs dill, or 1 to two dill plant
life four clean grape or horseradish
leaves

Pour the water right into a big pitcher or different vessel with a spout. Add the salt and stir to dissolve. Let cool to room temperature, then upload the vinegar.

Meanwhile, put together the cucumbers. In a big container, soak the cucumbers in bloodless water to cowl for 30 mins. Remove from the water and thoroughly test every one for bruising. Discard any that aren't as much as snuff. Trim away any remnants from the blossom ends and make certain the cucumbers are squeaky clean. Any undesirable factors can damage a whole batch. Drain the wiped clean cucumbers in a colander. Measure the mustard seeds, peppercorns, coriander, and allspice collectively right into a small bowl and blend well. Break the bay leaf and cayenne chile every into thirds. Have the garlic and dill ready.

Place a grape leaf in the bottom of a 1-gallon (3.8 L) jar or crock. Arrange one-third of the cucumbers on top of the leaf. Add one-third of the mixed spices, 1 garlic clove, 1 or 2 sprigs of dill, and 1 piece each of bay and cayenne. Follow with another grape leaf and another layer of cucumbers and seasonings, and then repeat with the third leaf and a third layer. You want to distribute the seasonings evenly throughout, but don't stress out about being too exact. Top with the remaining grape leaf. Pour the cooled brine over the cucumbers to cover. Weight the cucumbers so that they stay submerged in the brine. We generally use a small ceramic plate, sometimes topped with a small jar of water for additional weight, although some crocks come equipped with fitted stones specially made for the job. Lid the jar or crock and store in a cool, preferably dark location.

Check the pickles after four or five days. A skinny layer of white movie may

seem at the pinnacle of the brine. This is a herbal spinoff of the fermentation and may be skimmed off. Using tongs, eliminate a pickle and taste. It need to be mildly bitter or 1/2 of bitter. If you experience this diploma of sourness, you could refrigerate the pickles right now to gradual the fermentation. For stronger-flavored, brinier pickles, retain to ferment the pickles at room temperature for an extra four or five days.

Keep the completed pickles refrigerated. Although they may maintain for approximately three months, they're optimum all through their first month. Over time they'll turn out to be much less crunchy, however will nonetheless be delicious.

PICKLED RED ONION RINGS

Perky pickled purple onions are a satisfied addition to any plate. Strew them over a birria taco, toss them into salads, lay them atop your Ugly Burger or tuck them into your favourite sandwich to feature a smelly bite. This easy brine also can be used to pickle pearl onions, a exquisite addition to cocktails.

MAKES ABOUT I QUART (I L) JAR
three big purple onions, sliced into earrings approximately ⅛ inch (three mm) thick 2 cups (480 ml) purple wine vinegar
⅓ cup (sixty five g) sugar
2 teaspoons first-rate sea salt
3 or four sprigs marjoram or
thyme three allspice berries
I clean or dried chile (optional)

Place the sliced onions in a 1-quart (1 L) jar. In a small saucepan, integrate the vinegar, sugar, and salt and produce to a simmer over medium heat, stirring to dissolve the sugar. Add the marjoram, allspice, and chile and simmer for two mins longer. Carefully pour the recent brine over the onions and allow cool to room temperature.

Cover and refrigerate in a single day earlier than serving. Although those onions will maintain refrigerated for numerous months, they're at their quality all through the primary four weeks.

From left: Loulou's Garden Sweet-and-Savory Fruits, Cherry Mostarda, Bread and Butter
Pickles, Cherry Mostarda, Green Tomato Chutney, Classic Cucumber Dills, Marinated
Olives, Pickled Red Onion Rings

LOULOU'S GARDEN SWEETAND-SAVORY FRUITS

We first commenced promoting our charcuterie on the Saturday farmers' marketplace in Berkeley at a stand simply round the corner to Casey Havre, proprietress of Loulou's Garden and maker of wonderful jams, pickles, and preserves. This recipe became passed down from Casey's exquisite-aunt Louise, who might put together it together along with her very own home-grown figs, dried withinside the cellar. As a treat, Aunt Louise might wrap a slice of salami across the sweet-and-savory figs for younger Casey.

We love this sweet-and-savory concoction paired with salami and different cured or smoked meats, too. Once the end result are completed, lessen any leftover brine to a syrupy consistency and drizzle over grilled beef or duck.

MAKES 2 PINT (480 ML) JARS
three cups (360 ml) pink wine vinegar
½ cup (one hundred twenty ml) balsamic vinegar
½ cup (one hundred seventy g) honey
I cup (a hundred and fifty g) dried figs
½ cup (seventy five g) raisins
I cup (a hundred thirty g) dried apricots
I cup (a hundred and eighty g)
dried pear halves four árbol
chiles
three or four cloves garlic, peeled
however left complete 2 dried bay
leaves
2 small cinnamon sticks, or I big cinnamon stick, damaged
in 1/2 of

In a saucepan, integrate the vinegars and honey, region over medium warmness, and produce to a simmer to dissolve the honey.

Loosely percent the figs, raisins, apricots, and pears into 2 easy pint (480 ml) jars, setting approximately one-fourth of the fruit in every jar. Add 1/2 of of the chiles, garlic, bay, and cinnamon. Add the closing end result

to the jars, dividing them calmly and leaving ½-inch (12 mm) headspace on the top. Slowly pour the new vinegar syrup over the end result, immersing them absolutely. Release any air bubbles with the aid of using lightly prodding the fruit with a chopstick.

Lid the jars and refrigerate. Allow the end result to macerate for as a minimum 1 week earlier than serving. The end result will hold nicely refrigerated for up to two months. Alternatively, after screwing at the lids, technique the jars in a hot-water tubtub for 20 mins as instructed, then save in a groovy cabinet for up to at least one year, refrigerating the jars when they had been opened.

MARINATED OLIVES

A few slices of Saucisse Sec aux Herbes de Provence, a tumbler of pastis, and a bowl of those olives are the subsequent pleasant aspect to a holiday at the French Riviera. Warming the fragrant garlic, spices, and citrus withinside the olive oil permits the flavors to bloom. Be positive to serve those olives at room temperature or barely warmed.

MAKES ABOUT THREE CUPS (430 G)
3 cups (430 g) blended olives (which include picholine, tournante, Gaeta, niçoise, and Arbequina)
½ cup (one hundred twenty ml) olive oil I
dried cayenne chile
½ teaspoon fennel seeds, toasted
three cloves garlic, gently crushed
I dried bay leaf
I sprig thyme
Wide strips of zest of one lemon or orange
½ cup (one hundred twenty ml) dry white wine

Place the olives in a colander and rinse in brief below cool going for walks water. In a small saucepan, integrate the olive oil, chile, fennel seeds, garlic, bay, thyme, and zest. Place over low warmness and warmth lightly for five mins, then stir withinside the olives simply to warm.

Turn off the warmth and upload the white wine. Let cool barely earlier than serving or refrigerate for later use. Although they'll hold nicely refrigerated, they may be pleasant eaten inside three weeks.

ROOT VEGETABLE CHOWCHOW

Chowchow is a candy-and-highly spiced blended-vegetable pickle ideal for topping a sausage sandwich or for taking part in along smoked or grilled meats. Although commonly made with a mix

of summer vegetables such as cucumbers, green tomatoes, and sweet peppers, Chris Lohman, our resident country boy and pickle aficionado, developed this recipe to take advantage of sweet, crunchy root vegetables in the winter months.

MAKES 2 QUART (2 L) JARS
1 cup (one hundred twenty g) peeled and julienned carrot 1 cup (one hundred twenty g) peeled and julienned turnip
1 cup (120g) peeled and julienned rutabaga
1 cup (one hundred twenty g) peeled and julienned celery root 1 cup (one hundred twenty g) peeled and julienned daikon
2 cups (240 g) peeled and julienned goldenbeet
2 cups (a hundred and forty g) thinly sliced inexperienced cabbage
1 yellow onion, thinly sliced
1 tablespoon pleasant sea salt
2 cups (480 ml) cider vinegar, plus greater ifneeded 1 cup (240 ml) water
1 cup (2 hundred g) sugar
2 teaspoons chile flakes
2 teaspoons complete yellow mustard seeds
1½ teaspoons floor yellow mustard seeds 1 teaspoon celery seeds
1 teaspoon floor turmeric

In a big colander, toss collectively the carrot, turnip, rutabaga, celery root, daikon, beet, cabbage, and onion. Add the salt and lightly rubdown into the greens to inspire the discharge of water. Set the colander over a bowl, cowl with plastic wrap, and refrigerate overnight.

The following day, percent the greens into 2 easy quart (liter) jars. Discard any liquid that has collected withinside the bowl.

To make the brine, in a saucepan, integrate the two cups (480 ml) vinegar, water, sugar, chile flakes, complete and floor mustard seeds, celery seeds, and turmeric. Place over medium warmness and produce to a rolling boil, then eliminate from the warmth.

Carefully pour the brine into the jars. Make positive the greens are completely submerged in brine. Top the jars with extra vinegar, if necessary. Lid the jars tightly. After they have got cooled sufficient to handle, flip the jars the wrong way up and maintain to chill absolutely to room temperature.

Place the jar upright withinside the fridge to store. It is first-rate to permit the chowchow take a seat down for some days earlier than the use of to permit the flavors to develop. It will preserve withinside the fridge for approximately 1 month.

TRADITIONAL SAUERKRAUT

Crunchy, tangy, clearly fermented sauerkraut is a charcuterie staple, offering a counterpoint to the smoky, fatty meats in lots of traditional preparations, from Alsatian-fashion Choucroute Garni to a stacked pastrami sandwich.

Sauerkraut is certainly cabbage combined with salt, and making your personal sauerkraut is straightforward and satisfying. A strong stone crock is the most effective fermentation vessel on your kraut. Its thick stone partitions assist to preserve the kraut at a steady temperature. Some crocks, which include those made through German producer Harsch Gairtopf, are even geared up with weights designed to preserve the cabbage submerged in its brine and with a gutter round its rim that permits you to create an hermetic water seal. But we've additionally made many a first rate batch of sauerkraut the use of a bucket, a plate, a water jug, and a loosely knotted trash bag.

This recipe requires 10 pounds (four.five kg) of cabbage, which might also additionally look like a lot, however preserve in mind, as soon as salted, the cabbage loses quantity dramatically. If you would love to make greater or much less, simply make sure to apply three percentage salt through weight for some thing quantity of trimmed cabbage you pick out to apply.

MAKES ABOUT FOUR QUARTS (FOUR L)
10 pounds (four.five kg) inexperienced cabbage, outer leaves
removed, quartered thru the stem end, and cored
four.eight ounces (152 g) best sea salt
OPTIONAL SPICES
½ teaspoon yellow mustard seeds
1 teaspoon peppercorns
½ teaspoon allspice berries
2 or three entire cloves

Lightly rinse the trimmed cabbage beneathneath cool walking water. Slice crosswise into ribbons approximately ⅛ inch (three mm) wide. Place the sliced cabbage in a massive bowl or field and toss with the salt. To assist start the extraction of water, gently knead the salt into the cabbage.

When the cabbage starts offevolved to launch a few liquid, after approximately 30 minutes, % it right into a easy ceramic crock or bucket, a handful at a time, urgent down after every addition. When all the cabbage and its juices had been brought to the crock, weight the cabbage. If your crock does now no longer come geared up with equipped weights, use a heavy ceramic plate, crowned with a jug of water for added weight. Press down gently at the weights. The brine must upward push up at the least 1 inch (2.five cm) above the floor of the cabbage. If the cabbage has now no longer produced sufficient brine, you may upload 1 cup (240 ml) water combined with ½ teaspoon best sea salt to elevate the extent of the brine.

To preserve out undesirable elements, lid your crock, or in case your crock does now no longer have a lid, loosely cowl it with a massive trash bag. Store the crock in a cool, darkish location. A basement or storage is first-rate.

Check the crock each few days to make certain the brine stage remains nicely above the floor of the cabbage. Skim off any white foam that looks at the floor. Sauerkraut can deliver off a strong, every so often ugly scent at the same time as fermenting, which isn't indicative of the very last product. The fermentation typically takes approximately four weeks, however it is able to take much less time withinside the hotter months or greater at some point of cooler instances of the year. Taste the sauerkraut after 2 weeks and screen its progress. When it has executed a stage of sourness you enjoy, take away it from the crock, % it into easy glass jars, and refrigerate to arrest the fermentation. It will preserve nicely refrigerated for three to four months.

CHERRY MOSTARDA

Whenever we tour to Italy, we inventory up on olio essenziale di senape (important oil of mustard), the element that gives

mostarda di frutta, a conventional northern Italian accompaniment to boiled or roasted meats, its sharp zing. Essential oil of mustard isn't like the mustard oil normally offered in Indian groceries. It is concentrated, extraordinarily potent, and doubtlessly risky if used incorrectly. Outside northern Italy, this olio is unusual and noticeably regulated. We had been pretty fortunate on a current experience to stumble into the Antica Erboristeria Romana, a shoebox of a store someplace close to the attention of Rome's labyrinthine middle this is coated from ground to ceiling with curious shelves and tiny spicefilled drawers. When the owner reappeared from the lower back room with 3 tiny bottles and lots of Italian words (and gestures) of warning, we had been elated. *Mostarda could be at the menu!*

Even with out the few coveted drops of important oil of Mustard, this mostarda is a sweetly piquant foil to earthy salumi, decadent pâtés, and roasted duck or beef. It additionally makes an outstanding stuffing for beef loins and shoulders. Although cherries are a non-public favourite on this recipe, you may alternative apricots, peaches, nectarines, or peeled and diced pears for a in addition zesty concoction.

MAKES ABOUT 2 PINT (480 ML) JARS
1½ pounds (680 g) cherries
1½ cups (three hundred g)
sugar
⅓ cup (seventy five ml) white wine vinegar
¼ cup (forty g) yellow mustard seeds, gently toasted and floor
¼ cup (forty g) yellow mustard seeds, gently toasted
¾ teaspoon sea salt

½ teaspoon freshly floor pepper
1 or 2 drops vital oil of mustard (optional)

Stem and pit the cherries, booking the pits. Place the pits on a rectangular of cheesecloth, carry collectively the corners, and tie securely with wire to make a sachet (or use a muslin bag).

In a saucepan, integrate the sugar and vinegar over medium warmth and warmth, stirring to dissolve the sugar. Cook for approximately 10 mins, or

till syrupy. Add the cherries and the sachet and prepare dinner dinner for approximately 10 mins, till the fruit starts to soften. Add the floor and complete mustard seeds, prepare dinner dinner for two mins greater to thicken, then pull off the warmth.

Stir withinside the salt and pepper and thoroughly administer the drops of mustard oil. Let cool withinside the pan at room temperature. Remove and discard the sachet. Taste for seasonings and modify if necessary, then pour into easy pint jars and refrigerate. The mostarda continues properly refrigerated for two to three weeks. For longer storage, procedure the jars in a hot-water tubtub for 20 mins as instructed, then save in a fab cabinet for up to at least one year, refrigerating the jars after they had been opened.

GREEN TOMATO CHUTNEY

At the tail quit of tomato season, there's nearly constantly an abundance of inexperienced tomatoes that ought to be harvested earlier than the primary frost. After ingesting our fill of fried inexperienced tomato and bacon sandwiches, we flip the the rest into this delicately candy and highly spiced chutney. Slather it on a meat loaf sandwich, serve it along an collection of terrines, or stuff it interior a beef roast earlier than smoking or roasting.

MAKES ABOUT THREE PINT (480 ML) JARS
1 cup (240 ml) cider vinegar
1 cup (220 g) firmly packed darkish
brownsugar 2 cups (320 g) diced yellow
onion
½ cup (seventy five g) diced pink
candy pepper 2 dried cayenne chiles

2 teaspoons peeled and freshly grated ginger
1 tablespoon yellow mustard seeds
four allspice berries
2½ pounds (1.2 kg) inexperienced tomatoes, cored and reduce into big cubes
Fine sea salt

In a big saucepan, integrate the brown sugar and vinegar over medium warmth and produce to a Simmer, stirring to dissolve the sugar. Simmer, stirring occasionally, for approximately five mins, till thick and syrupy. Add the onion, candy pepper, chiles, ginger, mustard seeds, and allspice and simmer for five mins. Add the tomatoes, season with salt, and flip down the warmth to low. Cook, stirring occasionally, for approximately 12 to fifteen mins, till the tomatoes are softened and the aggregate is thick and jammy.

Taste and modify the seasonings if necessary. Pour into easy pint jars, permit cool, then cowl and and refrigerate. The chutney continues properly refrigerated for three to four weeks. For longer storage, procedure the jars in a hot-water tubtub for 20 mins as instructed, then save in a fab cabinet for up to at least one year, refrigerating the jars after they had been opened.

BLACK COFFEE AND BOURBON BARBECUE SAUCE

Strong black espresso and an extended pour of bourbon supply this fish fry sauce a bit backbone. It is vital for Pulled Pork and is a exceptional mop for any smoked beef, beef, or chicken. Use good-first-class espresso and bourbon and make certain to stir in any smoky meat drippings you've got got on hand.

MAKES ABOUT FOUR CUPS (960 ML)
1½ cups (360 ml) pink wine vinegar
1½ cups (360 ml) ketchup
1 cup (240 ml) beef broth (see Basic Rich Broth)
½ cup (a hundred and ten g) firmly packed darkish brown sugar

½ cup (a hundred and twenty ml) freshly brewed sturdy espresso
¼ cup (60 ml) bourbon
Smoked-meat pan drippings, for flavoring (optional)
Fine sea salt

In a saucepan, simmer the vinegar over medium warmth till decreased with the aid of using approximately half. Add the ketchup, broth, sugar, espresso, bourbon, and drippings, stir properly, and simmer, stirring frequently, for approximately 30 mins, till the flavors combination harmoniously. Remove from the warmth and season with salt.

Serve proper away, or permit cool, cowl, and refrigerate for up to at least one week.

CHILE TOMATO SAUCE

This candy and richly spiced sauce got here into being one September afternoon because of an overabundance of ripe tomatoes and peppers from our garden. It has turn out to be greater common than ketchup at our table, a go- to condiment for

tacos, lamb burgers, or grilled chicken. You also can stir it right into a easy red meat stew or simmer Lamb and Herb Meatballs in it.

MAKES ABOUT THREE PINT (480 ML) JARS
2½ pounds (1.2 kg) tomatoes
1 pound (450 g) crimson candy peppers
four to six ounces (a hundred and fifteen to one hundred seventy g) warm crimson chiles (inclusive of jalapeño or serrano)
1 huge yellow onion, quartered
6 cloves garlic, peeled however left
entire 1 teaspoon cumin seeds, toasted
½ teaspoon peppercorns, toasted
6 allspice berries

1 entire clove

¼ cup (60 ml) olive oil Fine sea salt

Preheat the broiler.

Place the tomatoes, peppers, chiles, onion, and garlic on a huge baking sheet. Slip the veggies below the broiler and broil, turning as had to shadeation evenly, for five to 7 mins, till the skins of the tomatoes, peppers, and chiles blister. Remove from the broiler and allow the veggies cool till they may be handled.

Peel and seed the tomatoes, peppers, and chiles. Working in batches, integrate the tomatoes, peppers, chiles, onion, and garlic in a meals processor and puree till smooth.

In a spice grinder, integrate the cumin, peppercorns, allspice, and clove and grind finely.

Heat the olive oil in a huge, robust pot over medium heat. Carefully pour withinside the puree, then upload the floor spices and season with salt. Stir nicely, flip down the warmth to low, and simmer for approximately 30 mins, till the sauce has thickened.

Pour the sauce into smooth glass jars, allow cool, then cowl and refrigerate. The sauce maintains nicely refrigerated for up to at least one week. For longer storage, method the jars in a warm-water tubtub for 20 mins as instructed, then shop in a fab cabinet for up to at least one year, refrigerating the jars when they had been opened.

HORSERADISH SALSA VERDE

Fresh horseradish root is gnarly, stupid brown, and really odorless. But whilst sparkling horseradish is peeled and grated, it produces a effective organosulfur compound, corresponding to mustard oil, which can clean the sinuses and convey on tears. It additionally provides a scrumptious kick to sauces paired with roasted and grilled meats, inclusive of this highly spiced model of salsa verde.

Choose horseradish roots which might be organization and wrinkle-free. Peel most effective as a great deal of root as you would like to grate, leaving the the rest intact. Freshly grated horseradish need to be used straight away or saved blanketed in vinegar to keep away from discoloration and bitterness.

MAKES ABOUT 2 CUPS (480 ML)

¾ cup (forty five g) chopped sparkling flat-leaf parsley
¼ cup (15 g) chopped sparkling oregano
¼ cup (35 g) rinsed and chopped capers
1 tablespoon garlic pounded to a paste in amortar with ¼
teaspoon excellent sea salt
2 tablespoons freshly grated horseradish
Grated zest and juice of one lemon
¾ cup (a hundred and eighty ml)
extra-virgin olive oil Fine sea salt

In a bowl, integrate the parsley, oregano, capers, garlic, horseradish, and lemon zest and blend nicely. Stir withinside the lemon juice and olive oil, then season with salt. Salsa Verde is first-rate served the identical day.

CÉLERI RÉMOULADE

Céleri rémoulade is as ubiquitous to the conventional French charcuterie as coleslaw is to the conventional American delicatessen. In this easy preparation, uncooked celery root is shredded and dressed with an assertive mayonnaise tempered with crème fraîche. Once you've got got peeled and julienned the celery root,

toss it straight away with the lemon juice, because it discolors quickly. This de rigueur salad is ideal for any picnic lunch or charcuterie unfold and makes a exceptional facet for sandwiches.

SERVES 6 TO 8
four celery roots, peeled and
julienned Fine sea salt
½ cup (one hundred twenty ml) freshly
squeezed lemon juice 1 egg
¾ cup (a hundred and eighty ml) olive oil
1 tablespoon garlic pounded to a paste in a mortar
½ cup (one hundred twenty ml) crème fraîche
⅓ cup (70 g) Dijon mustard
½ teaspoon freshly floor pepper
½ cup (30 g) chopped sparkling flat-leaf parsley

Season the celery root with salt, then toss with 2 tablespoons of the lemon juice. Transfer the celery root to a sieve located over a bowl and depart to weep even as you whisk collectively the dressing.

In a bowl, whisk the egg till blended. Very slowly whisk withinside the olive oil to emulsify. When the emulsion is thick, whisk withinside the garlic, the last 6 tablespoons (ninety ml) lemon juice, the crème fraîche, the mustard, and the pepper.

Discard any liquid that has gathered withinside the bowl below the sieve, then switch the celery root to the bowl. Pour approximately 1/2 of of the dressing into the bowl and blend with the aid of using hand to coat. Continue to feature dressing to flavor. You many now no longer want all of it. Fold in approximately two-thirds of the chopped parsley, then sprinkle the closing parsley over the pinnacle simply earlier than serving. This salad is is nice organized and served the identical day.

SIMPLE BEANS

Beans, in reality organized, are a splendid accompaniment to roasted and smoked meats. At the Fatted Calf, we put together beans nearly every day for salads, as a facet dish to revel in with our roasts, and for including to soups. We additionally promote a great quantity of dried heirloom beans for humans to prepare dinner dinner at domestic with sausages, ham hocks, and bacon. Our technique for cooking beans in all fairness easy: you need to start with accurate beans, ideally a flavorful heirloom variety, including cranberry, flageolet, Good Mother Stallard, or Yellow Indian Woman, and ideally now no longer extra than a 12 months old. Beans which have been sitting on the shop shelf or to your cabinet for too lengthy will now no longer flavor as scrumptious and are much more likely to prepare dinner dinner unevenly, ensuing in beans which can be crumbly or tough on the center. For perfect, creamy-textured beans each time, purchase beans from a very good supply and comply with this easy method.

MAKES ABOUT EIGHT CUPS (1.6 KG)
1 pound (450 g) dried beans

I tablespoon lard or pan drippings
I cup (a hundred and seventy g)
minced yellow onion I dried bay
leaf
Fine sea salt

Rinse the beans properly in numerous modifications of water, then vicinity in a massive bowl, upload water to cowl with the aid of using three to four inches (7.five to ten cm), and permit soak for as a minimum four hours or as much as overnight. Do now no longer soak beans for longer than 12 hours, as oversoaking can result in choppy cooking.

Preheat the oven to 300°F (150°C).

Choose a very good, ovenproof pot. Clay-pot fans will inform you that beans cooked in a clay bean pot are better, and we're willing to agree. But in case you do now no longer have a clay pot, a strong enameled solid iron pot or heavy Dutch oven additionally works properly. Ideally, the pot ought to be massive sufficient so that when the beans and water are in it, it's far more or less handiest 1/2 of complete to permit for growth and accurate air stream for the duration of cooking.

Set the pot at the range pinnacle over low warmness and upload the lard. When the lard is melted, upload the onion and lightly sweat for approximately 10 mins, till gentle and translucent. Drain the beans and upload them to the pot at the side of the bay leaf. Add sufficient water to cowl with the aid of using approximately 2 inches (five cm). Bring the pot to a simmer, cowl, and vicinity withinside the oven.

Monitor the development of the beans each half-hour for the primary hour, then each 15 mins after that. Different beans chefs at specific rates. Some beans prepare dinner dinner unexpectedly and might be carried out in much less than 1 hour. Others would require three hours or longer. Most fall someplace in between. If the extent of the water starts offevolved to drop and the beans are in chance of being exposed, upload extra water. When the beans start to melt however aren't pretty carried out, season with salt. Start with a small quantity, approximately 1½ teaspoons, then upload extra to flavor. Continue to prepare dinner dinner the beans till they're lightly cooked, with a creamy texture and gentle skin.

The beans may be served simply as they're, instantly from the pot with a drizzle of accurate olive oil and a handful of freshly chopped herbs, or they may be utilized in one of the following recipes. To shop the beans, allow them to cool of their cooking liquid after which refrigerate withinside the liquid for up to a few days.

COWBOY BEANS

The tiny purple pinquito bean, local to the Central California's Santa Maria Valley, makes a median pot of beans. Simmered with candy peppers and warm chiles, those beans are an excellent facet for grilled and smoked meats. Popular in the course of the western United States and northerly Mexico, they're at domestic with each fish fry and Mexican-stimulated dishes. You can replacement accurate-fine pinto or different small purple beans if the pinquitos show elusive. See photo.

SERVES EIGHT
I pound (450 g) dried Santa Maria pinquito beans, cooked as directed in Simple Beans
I cup (a hundred and forty g) finely diced bacon, home made or shop-bought
I white onion, diced
I purple candy pepper, seeded and
diced I tablespoon chopped garlic
I or 2 dried árbol chiles
Fine sea salt
I cup (250 g) tomato puree
I½ cups (360 ml) red meat broth (see Basic Rich
Broth) I sprig oregano
I sprig epazote (optional)

Have the beans prepared of their cooking liquid. Slowly render the bacon in a Dutch oven or clay pot over medium warmth. When the bacon releases a number of its fats and starts to brown, upload the onion, candy pepper, garlic, and chiles and stir well. Season gently with salt and prepare dinner dinner, stirring occasionally, for approximately 10 mins, till the onion and pepper are tender. Add the tomato puree, prepare dinner dinner for five mins longer, then upload the broth, oregano, and epazote.

Drain the cooked beans, booking their cooking liquid. Add the beans to the pot in conjunction with sufficient of the cooking liquid to cowl the beans through approximately ½ inch (12 mm). Bring to a simmer and regulate the seasonings if necessary. Turn down the warmth to low and simmer lightly for approximately forty five mins to marry the flavors. Alternatively, if the coals for your grill are glowing, the beans may be simmered over oblique warmth in which their taste will enjoy the fragrance of the wooden smoke. Serve hot.

Fagioli All'uccelletto

FAGIOLI ALL'UCCELLETTO

In Italian, an uccelletto is a "little bird." This charmingly named dish interprets to "beans cooked withinside the fashion of little birds."

Simmered in an herbaceous tomato and purple wine sauce with a touch of cured red meat, it's miles one of the maximum asked recipes on the Fatted Calf, in which we make it often to accompany roasted or braised meats. For a simple, hearty supper, upload some links

of Sausage Confit simply earlier than topping the beans with bread crumbs and baking.

SERVES 8
1 pound (450 g) dried borlotti, cranberry, or cannellini beans, cooked as directed in Simple Beans
1 cup (a hundred and forty g) finely diced pancetta or guanciale, homemade (see Pancetta Arrotolata or Guanciale) or store-bought
1 cup (a hundred and fifty g) finely diced yellow onion
½ cup (70 g) peeled and finely diced carrot
½ cup (70 g) finely diced celery or fennel
2 tablespoons minced garlic
1 dried cayenne chile
1 cup (240 ml) dry purple wine
1½ cups (375 g) tomato puree
1½ cups (360 ml) red meat or duck broth (see Basic Rich Broth) 2 tablespoons chopped clean savory
1 tablespoon chopped clean sage
2 cups (a hundred and fifteen g) clean bread crumbs
2 tablespoons pan drippings or lard

Preheat the oven to 300°F (a hundred and fifty°C).

Have the beans prepared of their cooking liquid. Slowly render the pancetta in a Dutch oven or clay pot over low warmth. When the pancetta releases a number of its fats and starts to brown, upload the onion, carrot, celery, garlic, and chile and stir well. Season gently with salt and prepare dinner dinner, stirring occasionally, for approximately 12 to fifteen mins, till the onion, carrot, and celery are tender. Pour withinside the wine and tomato puree and simmer till decreased through approximately one-third, then upload the broth, savory, and sage.

Drain the cooked beans, booking their cooking liquid. Add the beans to the pot in conjunction with sufficient of the cooking liquid to cowl the beans through approximately ½ inch (12 mm). Bring to a simmer and regulate the seasonings if necessary.

In a small saucepan, soften the drippings over low warmth. Add the bread crumbs and stir to coat. Spoon the bread crumbs flippantly over

the beans. Transfer the pot, uncovered, to the oven and bake for approximately 1 hour, till the bread crumbs are golden brown. Serve hot.

BUTCHER SHOP LINGO

Butterflied: This time period is used to explain a reduce of meat this is sliced almost in half, parallel to the slicing board, leaving a small hinge on one aspect that lets in the beef to be opened like a book (or the wings of a butterfly). This approach is frequently used to create a pocket for stuffings.

Caveman or Flintstone Chop: A thick pork or red meat loin chop with the rib and a part of the stomach nevertheless attached.

Certified Humane: A certification and labeling software designed to make certain that animals raised for meals are dealt with humanely during their whole lives, from beginning to slaughter. The requirements that ought to be met consist of a nutritious, healthy eating regimen with out antibiotics or hormones, get entry to to shelter, enough area to transport freely, the capacity to interact in herbal behaviors, and a low-pressure slaughter.

Dry Aging: A manner wherein meat (most usually pork) is hung in a cold, managed surroundings for a length of time (normally numerous weeks) to enhance taste and texture. During dry aging, herbal enzymes wreck down the connective tissue and inspire lack of a few moisture, which concentrates the taste.

English Cut: Term normally carried out to lamb chops reduce via each aspects of the spine and loin. It also can discuss with different forte butchers' cuts from the United Kingdom.

Farce: Also called forcemeat. A combination of chopped or floor uncooked meat and fats used to make sausage, salami, galantines, terrines, pâtés, loaves, or different meaty preparations.

Free-Range or Free Roaming: Term normally used to explain fowl that has been allowed get entry to to the outside for a part of its existence however isn't always always pastured or raised outdoors.

Frenched: Describes a bone-in reduce of meat (usually a rack or chop) that has been trimmed to reveal the bone for the sake of look sake most effective.

Glove-boned: Also called semiboneless. A time period used to explain quail or small birds which have had all in their bones, besides for the tiny wing and leg bones, removed.

Grain Finished: The exercise of feeding farm animals and different ruminants grain (commonly reasonably-priced corn or soybeans on large manufacturing unit farms or feedlots, however on occasion greater herbal grains, consisting of barley and rice, on smaller-scale operations) to enhance the taste and boom the fats content material of the beef.

Grass Fed: Describes the traditional, slow-developing approach of permitting ruminants (farm animals, sheep, and goats) to graze on clean pasture to advantage the fitness and fine of existence of the animals and to provide meat this is greater wholesome and greater herbal.

Halal: Term used for meals merchandise which are organized in keeping with Islamic regulation and below Islamic authority. It prescribes a particular approach of slaughter that requires creating a deep incision withinside the throat to reduce the carotid artery, windpipe, and jugular vein after which bleeding the animal absolutely earlier than processing.

Heritage: A breed of farm animal with unique traits now no longer appropriate to extensive present day farming and consequently endangered or rare. Hormone- and Antibiotic-Free: A tough to affirm declare made via way of means of the manufacturer that no hormones or antibiotics had been administered to the animal.

Kosher: Term used for meals merchandise which are organized in keeping with Jewish regulation and below rabbinical supervision. It prescribes that animals be slaughtered via way of means of a single, specific reduce throughout the throat, which reasons the animal to bleed to death.

Natural: Term used to explain a product containing no synthetic element or brought shadeation this is most effective minimally processed (or processed in a manner that doesn't essentially modify the product).

Organic: Term that suggests that the meals has been produced thru authorized techniques that combine cultural, biological, and mechanical practices that foster biking of resources, sell ecological balance, and preserve biodiversity and avoids using artificial fertilizers, sewage sludge, irradiation, and genetic engineering.

Pastured: Term implemented to animals which are raised commonly outdoors, wherein they could roam freely in a herbal surroundings and graze on grasses or forage for plants, insects, roots and different foods. This exercise guarantees a higher existence for the animals, limits environmental pollution, and yields meat and dairy this is greater herbal, nutritious, and higher tasting than what's produced on manufacturing unit farms.

Porterhouse Chop: A red meat, pork, or lamb chop that consists of the pinnacle of the loin in addition to a number of the tenderloin or fillet. Some parents recollect this chop the quality of each worlds.

Poussin: A younger chicken, usually four to six weeks old.

Primal Cut: A huge segment of meat this is separated from the carcass at some stage in butchering and from which retail cuts are fabricated.

Prime, Choice, and Select: Designations withinside the voluntary USDA grading machine for and via way of means of the red meat industry, wherein federal inspectors assign a fine grade to every red meat carcass at some stage in processing. Prime is the quality grade, preference is good, and pick out is acceptable; beneathneath this is the stuff that is going into processed and puppy foods. The awarding of grades is primarily based totally on the quantity of marbling withinside the meat and the age of the

animal, with the aim of making requirements of fine in marketing. Many grass-fed red meat manufacturers eschew this machine as it prizes grain completing and does now no longer do not forget the general fitness of the animal.

Silver Skin: The skinny layer of white or silver-coloured connective tissue discovered on the beef of red meat, pork, and lamb.

Spatchcock: A butchering technique (aka spattlecock) that eliminates the spine from fowl or sport with a purpose to flatten the frame in guidance for grilling or roasting.

Spring Lamb: A milk-fed lamb, commonly among three and five months old, that has born in past due iciness or early spring and taken to marketplace earlier than July 1.

T-Bone: A beef, pork, or lamb chop just like a porterhouse however with a smaller segment of loin attached.

Wet Aging: A deceptive advertising time period coined for meat this is saved in vacuum-sealed plastic bags (that is the enterprise norm, now no longer a technique) in place of dry aged.

Made in the USA
Las Vegas, NV
30 May 2024

90526400R10142